Prin[...]

Corporate Social Responsibility (CSR)

A guide for students and practicing managers in developing and emerging countries

EDITED BY:

David Katamba
Christoph Zipfel
David Haag
Charles Tushabomwe-Kazooba

Strategic Book Publishing and Rights Co.

Strategic Book Publishing and Rights Co.
12620 FM 1960, Suite A4-507
Houston, TX 77065
www.sbpra.com

ISBN: 978-1-61204-484-2

Typography and page composition by J. K. Eckert & Company, Inc.

We dedicate this book to all the students, practicing managers, civil society organizations, companies, foundations, and development agencies that have committed themselves to ensure the existence and prevalence of corporate social responsibility.

Special tribute to Mrs. Jean Hensley Kekaramu, who never saw the final output of this book. She died on Friday, 25th November, 2011, just before this book was out of production.

Contents

Foreword

The 20th Century leading Management Guru, Peter Drucker, once said *business should not only address problems of society but should also ensure that its activities that impact on society negatively are addressed.* Drucker's views contrasted with the views then that business had no business with society's problems. This view only led to the increasing demand by society on business not only to do good on society but to ensure that it did not impact on society negatively. This highlights the importance of Corporate Social Responsibility (CSR).

Today CSR is not philanthropy. It is a conscious effort by organizations to make sure that they address the challenges that society faces. CSR is bordering sustainable development where business not only act responsibly in terms of ensuring sustainability of resources but also generally improving society where the businesses exists. There is demand now that all businesses incorporate CSR in their strategies. This book gives an overview of CSR and provides an understanding of the practice of CSR not only for students but also for practicing managers. The book indicates how CSR can be incorporated into strategies of organizations, how CSR can be implemented, and also has insights into international practices.

I wish to pay tribute to the authors primarily Mr. David Katamba whose life in the most recent years has evolved CSR. He has championed it, he has lived it, and he is now writing about it. My congratulations to the authors and publishers of this book, *"Principles of Corporate Social Responsibility: A guide for students and practicing managers in developing and emerging countries."*

Prof. Waswa Balunywa (PhD)

Principal,

Makerere University Business School (MUBS)

Acknowledgments

The CSR Consultative Group would like to extend its sincere appreciation to all individuals who conducted research for the development of this book—Principles of Corporate Social Responsibility (CSR). These include: Mr. David Katamba, Dr. Isaac Newton Kayongo, Mr. Samuel Musigire, Ms. Jean Kekaramu (R.I.P.), Ms. Annet Nabatanzi Muyimba, and Ms. Irene Namutebi. All are staff of the Makerere University Business School (MUBS), Dr. Charles Tushabomwe-Kazooba (from Mbarara University of Science and Technology—MUST), and Mr. Babiiha Mpisi Sulayman (from Gulu University).

We thank David Katamba, Chairman of the CSR Consultative Group (CCG) and the Uganda Chapter for Corporate Social Responsibility Initiatives (UCCSRI) for coordinating the writing and publishing. The CSR Consultative Group also highly appreciates the German government and its support through the Deutsche Gesellschaft fuer Internationale Zusammenarbeit (GIZ) GmbH development agency, which provided the generous funding and technical support that made writing this book a reality. Special thanks go to Mr. Bodo Immink (Ugandan Country Director), and also to Dr. Christoph Zipfel (CSR/PPP Advisor) for his technical advice, collaboration and input during the entire process of the book's writing and development.

We also thank a team of reviewers and editors for this book. These are: David Katamba, Dr. Christoph Zipfel, David Haag and Dr. Charles Tushabomwe-Kazooba, Dr. Cedric Marvin Nkiko, and Prof. Dr. Geoffrey Bakunda.

Additional thanks go to the Research Assistant Mr.Tenywa Hamid who organized the various chapters into the final document.

We thank Mrs. Sabine Gisch-Boie. While still working as a PPP-CSR Coordinator at GIZ, she inspired the editors to the process of writing this book. She welcomed an idea that a "CSR curriculum ought to be developed in Uganda, with possibility of extending it to other related countries."

Lastly, exceptional thanks to Prof. Dr. Waswa J. Balunywa and Prof. Dr. Samuel Sejjaaka, being respectively Principal and Deputy Principal of Makerere University Business School (MUBS) for their personal support to the publication of this book and to the lead editor of this book to ensure CSR knowledge development in Uganda.

About the Editors

David Katamba (B.com, Msc. Marketing, CIM), is the founder and Chairman, Uganda Chapter for Corporate Social Responsibility Initiatives Ltd (UCCSRI), a leading not-for-profit private company in Uganda that provides CSR information and advisory services. He is also the Chairman for CSR Consultative Group, a network in Uganda that brings together CSR Experts and organizations. He is a lecturer of Marketing and Management subjects in Makerere University Business School (MUBS). In addition, he is a Ugandan-based Aga Khan Development Network (AKDN) and International Business Leaders Forum (IBLF) distinguished Trainer and Advisor on CSR strategic development. His special training and knowledge in CSR was acquired from the World Bank Institute, New York (2004); and from IBLF and AKDN in Istanbul, Turkey (2010). With over seven years experience in corporate sustainability practices in the Private sector, David brings a mix of Marketing and strategic management knowledge to the field of understanding and practicing CSR, to make the so called "complex" concept of CSR easily understood by students and managers in developing and emerging markets. Currently, he is the team leader for a research project intended to come up with a "CSR assessment and Diagnostic tool for companies operating in Uganda"—a German government funded project. Lastly, he is a PhD student (CSR Management).

Email: dkatamba@uccsri.com / katambadavid@yahoo.co.uk

Dr. Christoph Zipfel (PhD in Behavioral Economics, and MSc. Organizational Psychology). He currently works as a CSR Consultant for the Deutsche Gesellschaft für Internationale Zusammenarbeit (GIZ) in Uganda. He is supporting the CSR Consultative Group with technical advice and helped to set up the Global Compact Local Network in Uganda. In addition Dr. Zipfel is conducting Public Private Partnership projects with companies from Uganda and Europe. Before joining GIZ, Dr. Zipfel worked as consultant and project manager for the top management consulting firm McKinsey & Company. He holds a PhD degree in Behavioral Economics and a Master's Degree in Organizational Psychology from the University of Tubingen, Germany, and an MBA from IE Business School, Spain.

Email: christoph.zipfel@giz.de

David Haag (B.A., MSc. International Business, MSc. Economics and Management) is CSR-consultant, specialized in the fields of CSR communications and strategy consulting. He is also co-founder of SNEEP (Student Network for Ethics in Economics and Practice), the biggest CSR network for students in Germany. He studied Philosophy and Economics at the University of Bayreuth, Germany, and International Business Studies at the University of Magdeburg, Germany, and Macquarie University, Sydney. After a traineeship in public relations at J+K Strategic Communications in Berlin, he worked in Uganda for the NGO Somero e.V. and as a freelance CSR consultant. Since November 2010, he has worked as a CSR-consultant at Akzente Consulting in Munich, Germany.

Email: dhaag0711@googlemail.com

Dr. Charles Tushabomwe-Kazooba possesses a PhD in Social and Environmental Accounting from Mbarara University of Science and Technology, Uganda. He is a senior lecturer at the Department of Management Sciences. He is a Bachelor of Commerce graduate of Makerere University, and an MBA graduate of the University of Birmingham. He is also a Chartered Certified Accountant (ACCA) and a member of The Institute of Certified Public Accountants of Uganda (CPA [U]). His professional experience includes university administration and teaching since December 1984. Working in the university, the public sector stimulated his interest in social and environmental accounting. Tushabomwe-Kazooba brings another twist to this book by intertwining social and environmental accounting, a new field that is at the heart of public and private accounting—since social, environmental and developmental aspects are also inter-linked and are major concerns for both governmental and non-governmental organizations. Since June 2000, he has been a lecturer at Mbarara University of Science and Technology in the field of accounting and auditing courses. Apart from teaching, he practices accounting and auditing, and he is a strong supporter of corporate social responsibility.

Email: tkazooba@gmail.com

About the Contributors

Isaac Newton Kayongo (MBA, Finance; PhD, Finance). Dr. Kayongo is the Head of Department (HOD) of Leadership and Governance. His area of interest is Finance and Banking. He has been a Business Manager at Bugema College, now Bugema University (an equivalent to Deputy Vice Chancellor, Finance). He lectured at Nkumba University before coming to MUBS where he joined as a lecturer under the Department of Finance, and he subsequently promoted to the position of HOD in August 2006. He is also a Council Member of Bugema University, in addition to serving on the education committee of the Institute of Corporate Governance of Uganda (ICGU).

Email: isaackayongo@yahoo.com

Annet Nabatanzi Kabugo Muyimba (MSc. Marketing, MCIM, B.COM, PhD candidate). She heads the Marketing and International Business department at Makerere University Business School (MUBS). Her research interests are mainly in Service Marketing, Export and Agri-business Marketing, Branding and Enterprises competitiveness. She has more than ten years experience in lecturing, training and consultancy in various areas of marketing, SMEs, Export and Agri-business development. Major conferences in which she has presented include: MUBS AIMC, ORSEA, IAABD, AICE South Africa; Whitman Conference Syracuse University, New York. She is winner of Best Paper- SAICE 2009 in South Africa.

E-mail: anmuyimba@yahoo.com

Babiiha Mpisi Sulayman (MA Ethics and Development Studies, PGDE, BA (Hons), PhD Candidate) obtained a Bachelor's degree and a Post Graduate Diploma in Education at Makerere University, Kampala in 1984 before joining Uganda Martyrs University, Nkozi for the

MA degree in 1998. He has served in the education sector at various levels as an educator, administrator, and as a civil society activist. Currently, he is Deputy Dean, Faculty of Business and Development Studies at Gulu University, northern Uganda. And since 2005, Mr Babiiha has also been the Publicity Secretary of Uganda Development Studies Association (UDESA), an organization that brings together both academics and practitioners in development in Uganda.

Mr. Babiiha brings a wealth of experience both as an educationist and a civil society activist. His long-standing ties with the local communities: as Chairman, Toro Muslim District up to 2005; and Executive Secretary of Kasese Muslim Education Centre, western Uganda from 1998 to date, introduced him to corporate social responsibility in the aftermath of the political insurgency in western Uganda. His efforts in lobbying and advocacy for various forms of support to the local communities in the Rwenzori sub-region following the war between the Allied Democratic Forces (ADF) and the Uganda Peoples' Defence Forces (UPDF) gave him the impetus to delve into the theory and practice of corporate social responsibility.

Email: s.m.babiiha@gu.ac.ug; sbabiiha@yahoo.com

Irene Namutebi (MSc. Human Resource Management, BBA). She is a Senior Administrative staff of Makerere University Business School (MUBS). She has professional experience in public university administration from 2001 to the present. She is a member of the Young Professional Managers Association, an organization whose major focus is to train young managers in management and leadership skills, one of which is strategic corporate behavior and Corporate Social Responsibility. Currently she is working with this book's authors on a project to develop a "CSR assessment and Diagnostic tool for companies operating in Uganda"—a German government funded project. Her major role is to develop human resources behavioral anchors for CSR aspects.

Email: inamutebi@yahoo.com

Jean Hensley Kekaramu (R.I.P.) (MSc. International Hospitality Management). She was a Humanities Lecturer with a special concentration in the hospitality industry. She held graduate training experience in hospitality management. Her knowledge and skills extended to a number of fields in the management and marketing analysis of hospitality and tourism markets. She facilitated in the Makerere University Business School (MUBS) as an academic staff for over 8 years with further training and continuous development in her specialty. Her strategic interests in CSR began four years ago, when she joined a research team of this book's lead author addressing "CSR perceptions in Uganda: approaches and needs of companies."

Samuel Musigire (MSc Marketing, CIM-Dip in Marketing, PhD candidate). He is a lecturer at Makerere University Business School (MUBS). His research interests are mainly in strategic marketing, services marketing, and financial services. He has twelve years experience in lecturing, training and consultancy in areas of marketing management, business competitiveness, marketing strategy, and services marketing. He has presented at an IAABD conference, attended ORSEA and MUBS AIMC conferences.

Email: musigires@yahoo.co.uk

Prof. Dr. Geoffrey Bakunda: (MBA and PhD in Business Competitiveness). His main area of expertise is in planning and strategic management and public-private sector partnerships promotion, and business and enterprise development with a particular focus on SMEs. He has researched, consulted and published for many years. Dr. Bakunda possesses extensive experience in capacity building and trade policy advocacy, cutting across a number of sectors. In addition, he has been actively involved in advocating for mainstreaming trade policy issues in the national development agenda and explicating the link between trade and poverty. He is the co-founder and Senior Policy Analyst with the African Centre for Trade and Development (ACTADE), a local NGO focusing on trade policy advocacy, trade information dissemination, capacity building and research. He has been a member of the Inter Institutional Trade Committee and the National Development Forum of the Ministry of Tourism Trade and Industry (MTTI) in Uganda for eight and three years respectively. He is very familiar with Government policy frameworks in general, as well as those on Trade and Private Sector Development and international frameworks on poverty reduction, and human development and private sector development. His latest international publication is entitled, "Understanding How Firms Relate to their Markets in Africa: The Case of Uganda."

Email: gbakunda@yahoo.com

Corresponding Contributors

Sabine Gisch-Boie: From 2007–2009, she worked as the PPP/CSR promoter of GiZ and coordinated the efforts that saw the initiation of the CSR Consultative Group. The development of a CSR curriculum (which further translated into one of the core textbooks) for Ugandan students and consequently for all students and managers in developing and emerging markets was one of her dreams, when working with GIZ in Uganda. Currently, she is the project manager for the establishment of a sustainable rattan supply chain in Laos, Cambodia and Vietnam (wwf.panda.org/rattan). Her interest in CSR rests in developing countries, as well as in establishing sustainable supply chains. She participated as a co-researcher on the first ever CSR research project in Uganda, "CSR in Uganda: Perceptions, approaches and needs of companies in Uganda."

Email: sabine.gisch-boie@gmx.net

Dr. Cedric M. Nkiko (PhD in CSR and Stakeholder Engagement). Dr. Nkiko is a Senior Sustainability Consultant with Derbyshire County Council's Stakeholder Engagement Division in the UK. In his role he enables the council to understand local communities better; to use research to inform health improvement needs and service delivery in commissioning; as well as forming effective partnerships with stakeholders to address inequality and to promote sustainable development. During the last five years, Dr. Nkiko has worked simultaneously with the WBCSD's initiatives that accelerate businesses' action to value and action toward sustainable development in this difficult economic climate. These initiatives have built on the WBCSD's expertise in sustainability reporting and accountability, where Dr. Nkiko has been an external sustainability consultant since 2004. Dr. Nkiko holds a DBA/PhD; MBA and BSc in Business Management, Finance and Sustainable Development. Dr. Nkiko is Ugandan, and throughout his career he has worked and lived in the USA, Switzerland, Brazil, South Africa, and Uganda, and is currently working in London, UK.

Email: cedric.marvin@yahoo.co.uk

List of Acronyms

BSR: Business for Social Responsibility

CC: Corporate Citizenship

CERES: Coalition for Environmentally Responsible Economies

CSR: Corporate Social Responsibility

DED: Deutscher Entwicklungsdienst (German Development Services)

EC: European Commission

EU: European Union

FUE: Federation of Uganda Employers

GOU: Government of Uganda

IBLF: International Business Leaders Forum

ICGU: Institute of Corporate Governance of Uganda

ICKM: International Conference on Knowledge Management

ISO: International Standardization Organization

LEU: Living Earth—Uganda

MUBS: Makerere University Business School

NEMA: National Environmental Management Authority

SME: Small and Medium-Sized Enterprises

UCCSRI: Uganda Chapter for Corporate Social Responsibility Initiatives

UIA: Uganda Investment Authority

UMA: Uganda Manufacturers Association

UNDP: United Nations Development Programme

WB: World Bank

WBCSD: World Business Council for Sustainable Development

Introduction

Principles of Corporate Social Responsibility (CSR): A guide for students and practicing managers in developing and emerging countries, is a book that can be used to teach a thirteen-week course unit at undergraduate level, or it can be used by practicing managers to understand the practice of CSR. It is founded on the premise that businesses and organizational activities are organized and conducted for the purpose of making money for their owners, as well as members of the public who have invested in the company (shareholders). The emerging concept of Corporate Social Responsibility (CSR), however, suggests that businesses and organizations also have obligations and responsibilities to the many other entities affected by their decisions. These entities are called "stakeholders" and include employees, suppliers, customers, communities and even the environment. Therefore, this course unit intends to equip students (who are the future) and current managers with skills of how to integrate CSR into their business strategy and operations. It starts with defining CSR, then shows how to get involved in CSR, communicating CSR activities to stakeholders and tracking CSR performance. It concludes by offering students practical skills in designing CSR strategies and using them for enhanced competitiveness, as well as tracking—assessing and measuring the performance of CSR programs. Students are also taught about international bodies that provide guidelines and benchmarks for CSR activities, the UN Global Compact, Global Reporting Initiatives, as examples.

LEARNING OUTCOMES

Students or managers who successfully complete this book should be able to perform the following:

1. Observe and integrate corporate social responsibility principles in their work places
2. Spread CSR awareness to others who have not had the opportunity to obtain it from this book or a class
3. Influence their organizations to adopt CSR in their core values and actually allocate a budget for its implementation
4. Link CSR to business strategy and see the competitive advantage of CSR for the company
5. Appreciate and participate in CSR activities in their communities
6. Promote ethical behavior both at their work place and among their communities

OBJECTIVES OF THE BOOK

1. To introduce the reader to the basics of corporate social responsibility
2. To equip the reader with the skills needed to integrate CSR into business decisions
3. To equip the reader with knowledge about CSR and enable them to become champions of CSR
4. To prepare the reader for future lessons and knowledge in the field of CSR

—David Katamba and Charles Tushabomwe-Kazooba

1

Corporate Social Responsibility: An Overview

David Katamba, Charles Tushabomwe-Kazooba,
Christoph Zipfel, and David Haag

1.1 INTRODUCTION

Corporate Social Responsibility, or CSR, as we shall from time to time call it throughout this book, is rapidly gaining importance as a business strategy. It has moved from being a "by the way" to a "must do" element in business planning. This implies that organizations need to have top-management commitment and a clear framework for implementing corporate social responsibility programs. Hence, CSR ought to be inherent in an organization's objective strategy. Renowned strategic management and business gurus like Kotler and Armstrong (2006), Stoner *et al.* (2003), and Porter and Kramer (2006) have already linked CSR with the competitiveness of a firm, so as to reinforce the concept's uniqueness and importance. In their article, "Strategy and Society," Porter and Kramer (2006) detail how to practice strategic CSR. Many other business practitioners as well as academicians like Carroll (1999), Visser (2008) and Katamba and Gisch-Boie (2008) have further underscored the need to integrate CSR into modern business and management. The challenge is now to know what CSR means and how it should be most effectively applied.

Whether it is your first time to hear about the concept of CSR or if you already had some vague knowledge about it, this chapter will help you to master its basics. The chapter takes you through various definitions of CSR and concludes with a note on how these converge to bring out a unified message. It also helps you to differentiate it from similar or related concepts. It concludes with a highlight of how CSR has evolved in Uganda.

CHAPTER OBJECTIVES AND LEARNING OUTCOMES:

At the end of this chapter the reader should be able to:

1. Demonstrate a clear understanding of the concept of corporate social responsibility.
2. List and differentiate the concepts that relate to corporate social responsibility
3. Apply the most relevant theories that explain corporate social responsibility as well as practices for their business.
4. Understand the status of corporate social responsibility in Uganda.

LIST OF SUBTOPICS IN THIS CHAPTER:

This chapter covers the following sub-topics:

1. Definition of and distinction between CSR and its related core concepts (philanthropy, sustainable business, corporate citizenship, business ethics, etc.)
2. Evolution of the corporate social responsibility concept and its brief theories
3. The evolution of corporate social responsibility in Uganda and its current position

1.2 DEFINITION OF CSR AND ITS DISTINCTION FROM OTHER RELATED CONCEPTS

1.2.1 Definition of CSR

The working definition of Corporate Social Responsibility (CSR) in this book is the one suggested by the European Union. Specifically, the European Commission (EC) states: "CSR is a concept whereby companies integrate social and environmental concerns in their business operations and in their interaction with their stakeholders on a voluntary basis" (EC, 2001). The definition from this source differs from others in this book or from other sources in the following respects:

- CSR covers social and environmental issues, despite the English term "corporate social responsibility." CSR is not or should not be separate from business strategy and operations. It is about integrating social and environmental concerns into business strategy and operations.

- CSR is a voluntary concept.
- CSR is how enterprises interact with their internal and external stakeholders (employees, customers, neighbors, nongovernmental organizations, public authorities, etc.).

For details about this adopted definition, its applicability, as well as other relevant documentation, the reader may find it useful to visit the European Commission website: http://www.eubusiness.com/topics/social/corporate-social-responsibility-in-the-eu

Although we have adopted the above definition, we nevertheless appreciate that there are a variety of other definitions for CSR (Stanwick and Stanwick, 2009 as example). In the end, however, the reader will realize that they almost always converge into one commonality. For example, Business for Social Responsibility (BSR) defines CSR as "achieving commercial success in ways that honor ethical values and respect people, communities, and the natural environment" (White, 2006). BSR points out that CSR is more than a collection of discrete practices or occasional gestures, or initiatives motivated by marketing, public relations or other business benefits. Rather, CSR is a comprehensive set of policies, practices and programs that are integrated throughout business operations and decision-making processes that are supported and rewarded by top management. According to the World Business Council for Sustainable Development (WBCSD, 2000, p. 9), "CSR is the continuing commitment by business to behave ethically and contribute to economic development while improving the quality of life of the workforce and their families as well as of the local community and society at large."

The definitions so far quoted (as well as others the reader may encounter) bring out a message that CSR goes beyond corporate giving, business or community relations, donations and corporate philanthropy. They further stress that an activity, to be branded as "CSR," should be a continuous commitment established by a business or organization—that is, it should not merely be an episodic endeavor. This means that if a company gives out t-shirts and jerseys to a football team today, then stops that next week and embarks on malaria mosquito nets donations, and then leaves that and pursues road safety campaigns, etc., they may not be regarded as a CSR-practicing company. There must be a continuous and, most importantly, a *strategic* commitment to an activity so that we may properly call it CSR. Given the example above, a company can therefore be involved in numerous social activities and still fall short of achieving CSR. We would only call it CSR if there is an underlying continuous and strategic commitment to social responsibility, and one which in the end will yield a positive impact for both the beneficiaries and the company itself. This means that strategic CSR involves the creation of a win-win situation and not just a one-sided win. By this we mean that the CSR-embracing firm should realize benefits if its CSR activities and efforts are to be sustained. Winning/benefiting on the side of a company stretches from short to medium and longer term benefits. These take different forms, such as costs reductions through energy savings and processes; improved reputation, customer loyalty, etc. For further details about the benefits, please read Chapter Two.

At this point, therefore, we can suggest to the reader that while there are a variety of definitions for CSR, or as the reader conceptualizes the concept of CSR, she or he should appreciate that some issues should not be ignored. That is, social, economic or environmental issues must appear in the definitions and conceptualizations, or in the interpretation of the concept of CSR. For example, in your attempt to understand or conceptualize CSR, the CSR definition of the EU encompasses social, environmental and economic aspects, the proactive involvement of stakeholders, as well as sustainability aspects (European Commission, 2002). Also Carroll's definition of CSR encompasses ethical, legal, philanthropic and economic considerations (Carroll, 1979; 1999), as does the WBCSD's definition.

To further simplify your understanding and conceptualization of the CSR concept, the proceedings of the ICKM (2005) may be useful. For example, in their paper, "Going beyond Corporate Social Responsibility in knowledge management," Reynaldo G. Segumpan and Joanna Soraya Abu Zahari helped to show the convergence of CSR definitions, conceptualizations, and views. They indicated that, from all perspectives, CSR is considered a form of business decision-making, ranging through business operations and discrete practice via a set of integrated policies, practices, and programs. CSR incorporates a business's commitment to quality-of-life of the workforce, its overall relationship with stakeholders, and its governance and accountability to stakeholders and the wider community. Therefore, CSR is a broader concept than often previously perceived, and this book will help you to explore it step-by-step. Briefly, however, the issues and practices most frequently cited as important in the context of CSR include: human rights (respect for employees, women's rights, child labor, and social justice), worker rights (health and safety, education and training, compensation and benefits), environment (protection inside and outside the physical facility, and legacies), community involvement (compliance with local laws, community assistance programs, and employee voluntarism), supplier relations (preferences for suppliers that adhere to some CSR principles, for example CERES), monitoring (management systems, accountability, reports, bonus on employment generation, and maintenance), and stakeholder rights (consumer rights).

1.2.2 Distinction of Corporate Social Responsibility from Other Related Concepts

CSR is often confused with other concepts, such as business ethics, cause-related marketing, philanthropy, and corporate citizenship. This section illustrates some distinctions and tries to clarify that these concepts are different, even though they may look similar.

i. Business Ethics

Crane and Matten (2007) define Business Ethics as "the study of business situations, activities, and decisions where issues of right and wrong are addressed." Thus, in contrast to CSR, business ethics offers a much broader perspective on ethics in the field of business and can be regarded as the fundamental theory underlying CSR or corporate citizenship. As a result of this hierarchical relationship, there are several dimensions of CSR that may link with Business Ethics. These include human rights, labor and security, enterprise and economic development, business standards and corporate governance, health promotion, education and leadership development, human disaster relief, and environmental issues.

ii. Cause-Related Marketing

Cause-Related Marketing most often appears as time-limited campaigns to link a specified worthy cause to the purchase of products or services. Often, a small part of the price will be contributed to the identified cause. In contrast to CSR activities, cause-related marketing is not based on strategic considerations, but is designed to create quick-wins for a company's marketing efforts. An organization with progressive CSR programs will demonstrate a long-term commitment to creating a win-win situation for the company and society—not only in the field of marketing, but throughout the value chain. Cause-Related Marketing describes the collaborative initiatives of a business and a nonprofit organization for mutual benefit. Businesses increasingly support initiatives or programs which directly or indirectly improve their own marketing opportunities.

iii. Philanthropy

There is also a difference between CSR and philanthropy. As Ethics in Action (2001) pointed out, CSR is going beyond voluntarism and charity. CSR practices reflect a company's commitment to carrying out its core operations in ways that create win-win situations for both the company and society. Therefore, in contrast to philanthropy, CSR comprises social responsibility for products, services and operations as well as charitable giving.

iv. Corporate Citizenship

In practice, Corporate Citizenship (CC) is also often presumed to be synonymous with CSR. However, there are some conceptual differences that should be highlighted. As Visser, *et al*, (2007) argue, in contrast to corporate social responsibility that the concept of CC perceives a company as being an actual member of society itself. Consequently, CC offers the view of a company as yet another citizen. Based upon that view, the scope of responsibilities a company has to address is much wider, as compared to CSR. According to Visser, *et al* (2007), CC can even be seen as "an aspirational metaphor for business to be part of developing a better world." Therefore, CC can be regarded as a more radical approach than CSR.

1.3 EVOLUTION OF STRATEGIC CSR AND ITS BRIEF THEORIES

1.3.1 Evolution of CSR

As used in this book, Strategic CSR means "fulfilling those philanthropic responsibilities which will benefit the business/company through positive publicity and goodwill" (Lantos, 2002, p. 206). According to Carroll (1996), strategic CSR was originally proposed in 1953, when Howard R. Bowen proposed that businesses have social responsibilities beyond those of economics alone. Bowen claimed that businesses also have a responsibility towards the wellbeing of society and its people—a "social responsibility," as he put it. His publication, "Social Responsibilities of the Businessman" was the first recognized academic work to address CSR. In it, he defined CSR more in terms of an obligatory business responsibility within the larger societal context. He specifically cited "the obligations of businessmen to pursue those policies, to make those decisions, or to follow those lines of action which are desirable in terms of the objectives and values of our society" (Bowen, 1953, p. 6). However, it was Archie B. Carroll who, in his definition of CSR, stated what he perceived to be the actual "social responsibilities" of a business: "The social responsibility of business encompasses the economic, legal, ethical and discretionary expectations that society has of organizations at a given point of time" (Carroll, 1979, p. 500). Wartick and Cochran (1985), in their attempt to conceptualize a model for Corporate Social Performance (CSP), redefined Carroll's (1979) four categories of social responsibilities as the Principles of CSR. Hence, according to Wartick and Cochran (1985), the value orientation of a company would form the foundation upon which it would formulate and manage its social responsibilities. Since publication of the work of Bowen and Carroll, in 1953 and 1979, respectively, many other practitioners and academicians—such as Porter, Freeman, McWilliams, and Siegel—have started to look at CSR more strategically, contending that CSR should indeed become an integral part of business. However, the reader should note that this positive discussion also attracted some dissenting scholars. Among them was the renowned economist Milton Friedman, who directly opposed its relevance—perhaps most pointedly in a 1970 New York Times article where he indicated that "the social responsibility of business is to increase its profits." However, in September 1970, Craig P. Dunn pointedly defended the relevance of CSR in business practice. By directly disputing Friedman's arguments, he showed why and how business entities should be more socially responsible. Friedman had claimed that if a business embraced CSR it would become more like a charity, and would not pay due allegiance to its shareholders. This view, however, was refuted by Dunn. In fact, Dunn stressed that unless a business was socially responsible, it might actually fail to even provide minimum returns to its share and stock holders. For a more detailed discussion of this debate the reader is encouraged to visit the following source for further clarification: http://www-rohan.sdsu.edu/faculty/dunnweb/rprnts.friedman.dunn.pdf.

With positive arguments such as these adding weight to the value of CSR practices, along with additional research findings, CSR has become a compelling strategic business tool and approach. This has been evident through various highly visible bodies such as Business for Social Responsibility (BSR), the United Nations Global Compact, the World Bank, the International Standards Organizations (ISO), and the International Business Leaders Forum. These organizations, and many more, have started crafting formal guidelines for integrating CSR into business strategy. Accordingly, the definition and under-standing of CSR has drastically changed and evolved since Bowen's 1953 conceptualization. Of considerable influence have been Freid-man's criticisms of 1970, Carroll's insightful articles (1979; 1999), and additional developments in more recent times when bodies like the EU (2000) and the WBCSD have come up with more formal and yet strategic definitions and guidelines to integrate the concept into business activities. Today, there is even a much broader and distinc-tive understanding of the strategic concept, as the reader may dis-cover when reading Porter and Kramer's (2006) article entitled, "Strategy and Society: The Link between Competitive Advantage and Corporate Social Responsibility."

1.3.2 Brief Theories to Analyze and Explain Corporate Social Responsibility

Business management, psychology, and all other disciplines use carefully constructed theories to explain and expand the available knowledge about the disciplines themselves. Similarly, CSR is also rooted in various theories, including stakeholder theory, social con-tract theory, and legitimacy theory. For detailed information, the reader is directed to Moir (2001). Brief summaries of each will be provided here.

i. Stakeholder Theory

Freeman (1984) proposed the concept of stakeholder theory. This theory claims that a corporation should not only consider the shareholders' interests, but also the interests of all stakeholders. Freeman defines a stakeholder as "any group or individual who can affect or is affected by the achievement of the organization's objectives." They consist of two categories: (1) primary stakeholders (whose absence in participation in the core activities of the firm leads to its collapse, such as shareholders and employees); and (2) secondary stakeholders (those affected by the organization, or who affect or influence the direction of the firm, but who are not directly involved in the company's transactions). A firm has a series of connections with different stakeholders and therefore has to decide which stakeholders should be treated with urgency and how to respond. A deeper analysis of stakeholder theory is not discussed here, as it is beyond the scope of this book. However, the reader is encouraged to read the article: "What do we mean by CSR?" by Moir (2001).

ii. Social Contract Theory

Gray and others (1996) as cited in Moir (2001) indicated that society can be conceptualized as a series of social contracts between the members of society and society itself. By this definition, businesses may be regarded as part of society and therefore should incorporate some degree of social morality in business behaviors. According to Moir (2001), morality consists of a set of rules governing how people are to treat one another, which rational people will agree to for their mutual benefit, on the condition that others follow those same rules as well. By this standard, businesses should be expected to provide some level of support to their local communities and have some degree of involvement in community activities. The social contract theorists agree with the stakeholder theorists that the interests of stakeholder groups are important, but they believe that those interests do not override non-stakeholder interests or demand such things as safety, health, freedom and prosperity.

iii. Legitimacy Theory

Legitimacy is "the societal perception that the actions of [a firm] an entity are desirable, proper or appropriate within socially constructed systems of norms, beliefs and definitions," Suchman (1995). For a firm to obtain legitimacy, Moir (2001) suggests that it must appreciate the need for meaningful corporate communications with society. He further indicates that an organization may adopt four broad legitimating strategies when faced with different legitimacy threats: (1) seek to educate its stakeholders about the organization's intentions to improve its performance; (2) seek to change the organization's perceptions of the event (but without changing the organization's actual performance); (3) distract (i.e., manipulate) attention away from the issue of concern; (4) seek to change external expectations about its performance. This theory best explains why firms should undertake CSR and also use CSR as a form of public relations.

Based on Moir (2001), we can conclude that these three theories are interlinked and effectively support each other. For example, to examine the practice of CSR within business, the principles described in social contract theory can be analyzed, with the aid of stakeholder analysis, to provide an enhanced reputation or greater legitimacy to the firm.

1.4 THE EVOLUTION OF CSR IN UGANDA AND ITS CURRENT POSITION

1.4.1 Evolution of CSR in Uganda

This particular section provides the reader with a working knowledge of how CSR has evolved in Uganda. For details about how it has evolved in a variety of other countries around the globe, refer to The World Guide to CSR (2010). This text is a collection of writings by over 30 practitioners and scholars, and was edited by Professor Wayne Visser. The book was published by GreenLeaf Publishing, London. Details can be obtained by visiting the publisher's website at: http://greenleaf-publishing.com/productdetail.kmod?productid=3097 or www.csrinternational.org.

The pursuit of socially responsible actions by businesses and business owners is not a new practice in Uganda. However, it is generally agreed that a "strategic approach" to such actions or practices is new in Uganda. Consequently, a review of the evolution of corporate social responsibility in Uganda is provided here.

Historically, Uganda has been well recognized for its hospitality and humanity as far back as the 17th century. Its earliest international business and trade activities can be traced back to the Slave Trade days, when the Arabs introduced Islam and "long distance trade." Years later, East African Coastal Trade (EACT)—which may have led to the emergence of the Swahili language—began to suppress the Slave Trade. Participants in EACT showed some awareness that humans should not be treated as slaves, and by 1807 both British and

East African courts began legislating against slavery. By 1879, the practice had been outlawed in East Africa. Later, just before entering the twentieth century, Uganda was colonized by Britain. This further modified various business and social activities, such as engaging suppliers forcefully in the production of raw materials (principally, coffee and cotton), and promoting western education through the construction of schools, etc. This continued with some form of "westernization" until Uganda's independence in 1962.

Regardless of the influence of the above mentioned factors (Arabs introducing Islam, trade and colonization), the Ugandan society followed the "African Traditional Society" (ATS) norms and beliefs. Nkiko and Katamba (2010) have indicated that theorists such as Okot P'bitek preached and campaigned for societal ethical values as early as 1950. They also indicate that acts of helping the deserving poor, of wealthy families taking care of orphans, and of creating awareness to protect human rights, among others, can be found in prehistoric literature. For example, when the missionaries came to Uganda in 1870s, they furthered the "western" way of living, including the construction of churches, schools and hospitals.

The roots of corporate social responsibility can be traced back further from the different cultural, religious and historical principles as well as philanthropic acts. For example, many different communities, especially in Central Uganda, formed into small welfare groups called "Muno Mukabi" that provided assistance during misfortunes such as the loss of loved ones or hardship following a bad harvest. In addition, common religious principles such as the Catholic "tithe" (the donation of one-tenth of personal income to the church), as well as the Muslim "Zakat" (the donation of 2.5—5% of one's earnings directly for the care of the poor), drew out almsgivings for the relief of the poor and disadvantaged.

The outcome of the African Traditional Society beliefs and western cultural influence created a significant economic and social impact during the 1950s. That is, some people started formal businesses and trade, although informal trading such as bartering was still in existence. As business boomed, there was a need to ensure sustainability and consequently competitiveness—so as to either have more businesses started or to better sustain the existing ones. In pursuit of this, Asians entered Uganda in 1960's. In the 1970's businesses started getting more involved in philanthropic practices, which one can view as building upon what the missionaries and the African forefathers had established during the African Traditional Society. Some of the socially responsible businesses of that time still continue, including Madhivani, Uganda Breweries Ltd. (now East African Breweries Ltd.), Kakira sugar works, etc. These companies have since moved on to formalize their philanthropic activities into sustainable "CSR" practices. They have expanded their activities from the "traditional philanthropic" operations to more strategic activities, in response to growing demands in their business environment. These demands include complying with the international export/import regulations throughout the supply chain and taking into account shareholder activism.

Therefore, many of the principles and ideas of CSR that have been carried out informally over many years, going back as far as the ATS, are being further modified and expanded today. Indeed, companies like Madhivani and MTN have set up entire foundations to manage their social responsibilities. Other companies have set up departments to handle CSR-related issues, while others have integrated it within their existing management functions—especially Marketing, Public Relations and Human Resources.

One of the major challenges for these companies, and many others, is that these activities have to be strategically integrated into their business practices. In some cases they have not been given the extra attention they deserve, so as to gain significant recognition (Katamba and Gisch-Boie, 2008). However, the attention given to CSR in Uganda is growing, and there are already companies that have proven CSR best-practice programs that may serve as role models for other companies. Just recently, in 2008, CSR-practicing companies such as MTN, BAT, EABL, UTL and Shell, among others, have been "evaluated" by the Government with the introduction of the "Investor of the Year" award under the theme of "Corporate Social responsibility." (See reports from the Uganda Investment Authority, 2009.)

Also different bodies have been set up by the government of Uganda to promote specific "CSR" components. For example, the National Environment Management Authority (NEMA) promotes environmental issues in Uganda, while the Directorate for Ethics and Integrity (DEI) promotes ethics transparency and accountability. The private sector is also free to supplement the government's efforts by setting up organizations that can proclaim and uphold the social responsibilities of business. For example, the Uganda National Consumers' Association pressures businesses to provide customers with high quality and safe products on the market.

Table 1   CSR at Uganda Telecom Ltd (UTL)

UTL is the leading provider of telecommunications services (both fixed and mobile networks) in Uganda. Its CSR initiatives include empowering the youth through educational programme sponsorships and leadership forums, running a child help line, and providing solar powered mobile recharge centres in areas of the country where the electrical grid has not yet reached. The company is well known for its philanthropic sports sponsorships and providing ICT for development. www.utl.co.ug

Source: Nkiko and Katamba (2010) in Word Guide to CSR.

1.4.2 The Current Position of CSR in Uganda

From the foregoing review we may observe that CSR is an increasingly broad concept. Companies and academics, as well as the government, are often failing to have a common understanding of what it stands for and how it should be carried out. Consequently, it is not surprising that there is no nationally applied and acceptable CSR model. However, a few models developed elsewhere are now being adopted in Uganda. For example, the UCCSRI study conducted by Katamba and Gisch-Boie (2008) observed that Freeman's stakeholder CSR dialogue model was the most dominate model used in Uganda, as compared to Carroll's CSR Pyramid.

In Katamba and Gisch-Boie's study, entitled "CSR in Uganda: Perceptions, approaches and needs of companies," businesses acted—either formally or informally, and individually or collectively—around the four internal and external elements of their stakeholders in areas of workplace, community, marketplace and environment. These businesses were not only accountable to their shareholders, but they also created a balance between and integration of stakeholders' interests that either affected or were affected by the firm's objectives. The study, however, also revealed that ethical and legal issues were mostly not adhered to in Uganda, since there is limited enforcement. This makes two elements of Carroll's model ("ethical" and "legal" responsibilities) applicable to a lesser extent. Thus, we can conclude, in the case of Uganda, that stakeholder theory is currently more applicable, as there is a possible natural fit between the idea of CSR and the company's stakeholders.

In consideration of this, further exploration into the stakeholder model was undertaken. It revealed that businesses in Uganda protect their main stakeholders interests in the workplace dimension (e.g., mainly employees) by putting into place policies such as employee equality and diversity, Health and Safety, HIV/AIDS policy, prohibition of child labor, etc. Regarding the community, businesses engage with society by making philanthropic donations toward important community developments such as education, health, infrastructure, sports, charities, culture and religion. The marketplace activities include all supply chain requirements as well as internal operations that prepare goods and services for the market. Concerning the environment, initiatives referring to renewable energy sources and efficiency, climate change, and management of emissions (effluents, waste, etc), as well as operations regarding land use and bio-diversity are brought forward by businesses—further supported and facilitated by the formation of a relevant government body, NEMA, in 1995.

1.5 CONCLUSION

The concept of CSR is widely interpreted and this has made it difficult for firms and practitioners to obtain a clear understanding of it. However, regardless of the varying interpretations, this chapter has emphasized that the meaning remains essentially the same. Also, socially responsible business is not a new practice anywhere in the world, though "strategic" CSR is a new and evolving concept. For example, in Uganda we have seen that it started way back in African Traditional society and has been steadily growing until today. Lastly, just like any discipline, the development and understanding of CSR is also guided by certain key theories.

1.6 LEARNING ASSIGNMENTS

1. Visit a company of choice—either physically, or by reading its current annual report or visiting its website. Read through its Vision and Mission statements and try to identify its different stakeholders. Design a CSR statement for such a company. Finally, citing reasons, indicate whether the company has a deep or vague understanding of CSR.

2. As there are a number of theories examining CSR, it can be very difficult to determine whether one particular theory is superior to the others. With reference to an analysis of the business practices in your country, indicate which theory you believe to be the most relevant or applicable.

Hint: In finding a solution to self check #2, above, it may be useful to read the article, "Positioning Stakeholders Theory Within the Debate on Corporate Social Responsibility," by Manuel Castelo Branco & Lucia Lima Rodrigues. Electronic Journal of Business ethics and organizational studies, Vol. 12, No. 1 (2007).

1.7 REFERENCES

Bowen, H. R. (1953), *Social Responsibilities of the Businessmen*, New York, Harper & Row.

Carroll, A. B. (1979). A Three-Dimensional Conceptual Model of Corporate Social Performance, in: *Academy of Management Review*, Vol. 4, No. 4, 497–505.

Carroll, A. B. (1987). *In Search of the Moral Manager*, Business Horizons, March–April, pp. 7–15.

Carroll, A. B. (1999). *Corporate Social Responsibility, Business and Society*, Vol. 38, No. 3, pp. 268–96.

Commission of the European Communities (2001), *Promoting a European Framework for Corporate Social Responsibility*, COM (2001) 366, Brussels.

Commission of the European Communities (2002), *Corporate Social Responsibility: A Business Contribution to Sustainable Development*, COM (2002) 347 final, Brussels.

Crane, A. and Matten, D. (2007), *Business Ethics*, Oxford University Press, Oxford.

EC (2001). *Promoting a European Framework for Corporate Social Responsibility, Green Paper*, European Commission, Directorate-General for Employment and Social Affairs, Bruxelles.

European Commission (2002). *Corporate Social Responsibility: A Business Contribution to Sustainable Development*, Office for Official Publications of the European Communities, Luxembourg.

Freeman, R. E. (1984). *Strategic Management: A Stakeholder Approach, Pitman Publishing*, Boston, MA.

Freeman, R. E. (1999). Divergent Stakeholder Theory, *Academy of Management Review*, Vol. 24, pp. 233–36.

Friedman, M. (1962), *Capitalism and Freedom*, University of Chicago Press, Chicago, IL.

Gray, R., Owen, D., Adams, C. (1996). *Accounting and Accountability; Changes and Challenges in Corporate Social and Environmental Reporting*, Prentice-Hall Europe, Harlow.

Katamba, D. and Gish-Boie, S. (2008). *CSR in Uganda: Perceptions, Approaches and Needs of Companies.* http://www.livinge-arth.org.uk/africa_programmes/uganda/CSR_study.pdf, accessed 20th January, 2009.

Kotler, P. and Armstrong, G. (2006). *Principles of Marketing.* 11th Ed. New Delhi: Prentice-Hall of India

Lantos, G. P. (2002). The ethicality of altruistic Corporate Social Responsibility, *Journal of Consumer Marketing,* Vol. 19, No. 3, pp. 205–230.

Moir, L. (2001). *What Do We Mean by Corporate Social Responsibility? Corporate Governance,* Vol. 1, No. 2, pp. 16–22.

Nkiko, C. M., and Katamba, D. (2010). *Uganda CSR Profile, in World Guide to CSR: A country by country analysis of corporate social sustainability and responsibility,* Edited by Wayne Visser and Nick Tolhurst, Green Leaf Publishers, UK, London.

Porter, M. E. and Kramer, M. R. (2006). Strategy and Society: The Link Between Competitive Advantage and Corporate Social Responsibility. *Harvard Business Review,* December 2006, 78–92

Stanwick, A. P. and Stanwick, D. S. (2009). *Understanding Business Ethics.* Canada: Pearson Prentice Hall

Stoner, F. A. J, Freeman, E. R. and Gilbert, Jr. R. D. (2003). *Management,* 6th Ed., New Delhi: Prentice-Hall of India Private Ltd

Suchman, M. C. (1995). Managing Legitimacy: Strategic and Institutional Approaches, *Academy of Management Review,* Vol. 20, pp. 571–610.

Visser, W. (2008). Corporate Social Responsibility (CSR) in Developing Countries, in: Crane, A., Matten, D., McWilliams, A., Moon, J., Siegel, D. (Eds.) *The Oxford Handbook Of Corporate Social Responsibility,* New York, Oxford University Press.

Visser, W., Matten, D., Pohl, M., and Tolhurst, N. (2007). *The A to Z of Corporate Social Responsibility,* Wiley Publishers, London.

Wartick, S. L. and Cochran, P. L. (1985). The Evolution of the Corporate Social Performance Model, *Academy of Management Review,* Vol. 10, No. 4, pp. 758–769.

White L. Allen (2006). *Business Brief: Intangibles and CSR. Business for Social Responsibility,* February 2006, p. 6.

World Business Council for Sustainable Development (WBCSD) (2000), *Corporate Social Responsibility, Making Good Business Sense,* January, 2000, p. 9.

2

Getting Involved in Corporate Social Responsibility

David Katamba and Jean Hensley Kekaramu

2.1 INTRODUCTION

This chapter builds upon information found in the previous chapter, Corporate Social Responsibility: An Overview. After evaluating the definitions, we explore how to get involved in CSR activities. Getting involved is the starting point of the integration of CSR into the business strategy and its implementation throughout a company's operations. This chapter, therefore, intends to provide basic information necessary to becoming meaningfully involved in CSR practices. That is: arguments for and against CSR, how CSR can enter organizations, CSR as a boardroom challenge, and top level management, involvement and endorsement. Issues on the relationship between CSR and leadership shall also be highlighted.

Furthermore, in this chapter, various options available for company involvement in CSR, and the potential benefits for engaging in CSR will be discussed. The material also provides for an analysis of situations where a company has involved itself in CSR and shows how to prepare and justify formal proposals for integrating CSR within the company.

CHAPTER OBJECTIVES AND LEARNING OUTCOMES:

At the end of this chapter, the reader should be able to:

1. Appreciate the reasons why companies need CSR
2. List the various options available for their company's involvement in CSR

3. Introduce to their company the potential corporate benefits under-lying CSR

4. Analyze their company's current and past operations and prepare formal proposals of how to integrate CSR into the next activities/decisions

5. Justify budgets for the company's involvement in CSR

SUBTOPICS TO BE COVERED IN THIS CHAPTER TWO ARE:

1. Benefits and Threats: Arguments for and against CSR

2. How CSR Enters a Company: CSR as a boardroom challenge

3. Corporate Social Responsibility and Leadership

4. CSR Dimensions Available for companies' involvement

2.2 ARGUMENTS FOR AND AGAINST CORPORATE SOCIAL RESPONSIBILITY

The subject of corporate social responsibility is surrounded by too much debate and criticism, especially that advanced by Friedman (1970). Proponents of corporate social responsibility argue that there is a strong business case for CSR, as corporations benefit in multiple ways by operating with a perspective broader and longer than their immediate short term profits. Critics argue that CSR distracts from the fundamental economic role of business.In his 1970 article, *'The social responsibility of business is to increase its profits,'* Friedman, a key cited ant-CSR proponent makes a preposition that CSR may to a certain point be irrelevant if the firm ethically pursues its profitability. To confirm this preposition, he indicates that maximizing profits must only be achieved while also,

"...conforming to the basic rules of the society, both those embodied in law and those embodied in ethical custom."

And that a business may:

"...increase its profits so long as it stays within the rules of the game, which is to say, engages in open and free competition without deception or fraud."

However, companies need CSR to lubricate the processes neces-sary for the attainment of their missions. This is because CSR further highlights and proves what the company stands for before its stake-holders. CSR's conceptual evolution, as well as the increasing number of companies that incorporate this strategic business approach, readily offer an initial argument to analyze CSR's benefits. Mittal, et al (2008) note, "Over the past decade, a growing number of companies have recognized the business benefits of CSR policies and practices." Levine (2008) highlights enhanced risk management as a main benefit of CSR in the short-term. Pro-CSR groups (for example the Bath Consultancy Group) successfully argue that CSR remains valid because it is also a positive way to enhance profits and meet stakeholder needs. Simon Cooper, an associate with Bath Consultancy Group notes that "...investors are seeing CSR as central to their assessment of their company's livelihood and success..." Bath Consultancy Group, no date).

At this point, it can be helpful to look at CSR in more general terms, specifically evaluating the arguments for and against CSR, so as to determine whether CSR is a "good/right" thing to do or not. This will be undertaken in the following subsections.

2.2.1 Potential Benefits of Corporate Social Responsibility to Companies

Potential benefits are sometimes treated as arguments for CSR. The scale and nature of CSR benefits for organizations may vary, depending upon the nature of enterprise. In certain circumstances it can be particularly difficult to quantify. Generally, depending on company perspectives, the following are benefits of CSR available to companies:

   a. **Human Resources:** CSR can be an aid to employee recruitment and retention (Battacharya, Sankar, and Korschun, 2008). Via the enhancement of reputation, retention of high quality employees can be more successful. Becoming a CSR eligible employer can maintain and enhance key personnel and investor confidence because CSR improves the working climate and thereby increases employee loyalty, motivation and productivity.
   b. **Risk Management:** Managing risk is a central part of many corporate strategies. Therefore, building a genuine culture of "doing the right thing" within a company can offset risks such as corruption scandals and environmental accidents (Kytle, Beth and Gerald, 2005).
   c. **Brand Differentiation:** In crowded market places, companies strive for a unique selling position that can separate them from their competitors in the minds of consumers. CSR plays a big role

in building customer loyalty based upon distinctive ethical values (Paluszek, 2005). Adherence to these values builds the company's reputation as a responsible business and is positively linked to an increased market share, as consumers increasingly include CSR criteria in their purchasing and service selection decisions. Recognizing this, Girod and Michael (2003) argue that CSR is "a key tool to create, develop and sustain differentiated brand names."

d. **License to Operate:** Companies are keen to avoid interference in their businesses through taxation or regulations. By taking various voluntary steps, companies can persuade governments and the wider public that they take issues such as health, safety, diversity, or the environment seriously. As good corporate citizens with respect to labor standards and their impact on the environment, companies can also reduce legal conflicts by utilizing CSR strategies to comply with various existing regulatory requirements.

2.2.2 Arguments against Corporate Social Responsibility

To this point we have examined various arguments in support of CSR. However, there are critics of CSR, including people of renown such as Milton Friedman (1970) who looks at making profits as the only CSR of a company. Worth noting is that even CSR proponents, like Bowen (1953) debate a number of concerns against CSR. Scholars above have indicated that if the purpose and nature of a certain business are questionable, then why should such a company engage in CSR? They highlight that in such cases, we could see concerns raised about insincerity and hypocrisy. Taking a closer look at Friedman (1970)'s arguments against CSR, we observe that the purpose of a business is to maximize returns to its share holders. Within a company, the adoption of CSR carries with it a cost increase and may impair performance. There are two categories of costs in relation to these, and these are management decision costs and operational costs. For example, a company practicing CSR needs to pay higher salaries to its staff, exhibits high security standards, and requires new energy saving devices.

Friendman (1970) further notes that managers need to take account of a wider range of goals and concerns, involve themselves in new and time consuming processes of consultation with outside stakeholders (since good CSR calls for stakeholder engagement), and must develop new accounting systems, monitoring, auditing among others.

Other scholars and managers have indicated that CSR is a dilution of companies' strategies, poses competitive disadvantages to companies, and predisposes failure for companies to take responsibility for issues that the government and other international bodies should be addressing. Consequently, CSR is criticized for degrading shareholder interests.

Whereas the authors of this book, and this chapter in particular, would like to leave the reader's and manager's mind unbiased in making a CSR involvement decision, an important point is made as follows:

Table 2   Point to Note

Despite the benefits matched against the "cost" of doing and or involving in CSR, we can recommend that CSR can be abandoned only if it does not make any impact for the organization or if it does not conform to the company's goals and objectives in terms of reputation, profitability and does not increase on its market share. Strategic involvement in CSR should yield a win-win situation, which is the backbone of sustainability of CSR undertakings.

2.3 CORPORATE SOCIAL RESPONSIBILITY AS A BOARDROOM CHALLENGE

Boardroom, in this book and chapter, refers to the topmost core meeting in which utmost and strategic decisions regarding a business'/firms' direction are made. The relationship, guidelines and bond that brings together the members that discuss business affairs in the boardroom can be referred to as Corporate Governance. This meeting is usually attended by the Board of Directors (BoD), top management staff, and/or shareholders. These participants are charged with determining the strategic direction and performance of an organization (Wheelen and Hunger, 2006). The capacity of those in the boardroom to make CSR-inclusive strategic decisions starts with their CSR knowledge and commitment, the applicable corporate governance principles in place, as well as the overall effectiveness of the Board of Directors (BOD). According to Terje, Vaaland and Morten (2007), CSR becomes a boardroom challenge because of the following:

i. The board has to ensure that a confidential information channel exists in an organization to ensure that crucial CSR information reaches top management of the company. Failure to create such channels will make this critical information fail to be acted on by the responsible persons in the organization hence rendering the organization's top management 'in-active.' Surprisingly such information may leak to the media in a negatively construed way which will damage the reputation of the firm (or its board). Lessons can be drawn from the case of Statoli (a Norwegian government oil and gas company) which entered into a contract which was on re-evaluation was found to be contrary to Statoli's ethics. The CEO was warned but kept a deaf ear. Thereafter the Chairman of the Board was informed, who also kept a deaf ear. Terje I. Vaaland and Morten Heide (2008) in their article, *"Managing corporate social responsibility: lessons from the oil industry,"* tell us that "...the incident accelerated when the leading business newspaper in Norway publicized the story. Shortly afterwards the vice-president for international operations was forced to leave the company. The Board then fired the CEO and finally the chairman of the board resigned."

ii. CSR management requires a system for identifying the most significant stakeholders (actors and their expectations).

iii. There is a need to develop resources such as sustainability reports, ethical guidelines and management control systems based on input from significant stakeholders, including whistle blowers, and as a learning benefit from past CSR incidents.

iv. Investments to enforce CSR require attention to both the long-term building of company reputation and the ability to handle unexpected CSR incidents in a systematic and professional manner.

When potentially critical incidents arise, the board must always allow the internal tools to function as intended (see Table 3).

2.4 CORPORATE SOCIAL RESPONSIBILITY AND LEADERSHIP

According to BNET Business Directory, Leadership is "the capacity to establish direction, to influence and align others toward a common goal, motivating and committing them to action and making them responsible for their performance." This means that, "Leadership is ultimately about creating a way for people to contribute to making something extraordinary happen" (Kouzes and Posner, 2007). In modern management, it has been observed that it is not all about mere leadership. It is about "effective leadership." Therefore, effective leadership is the ability to successfully inte-

Table 3   CSR As a Boardroom Challenge

While any CSR undertaking "must have" a boardroom or top management approval, the CSR challenge in the boardroom starts from the fact that there is always a difference in the quality of Board/top management members. Some of them are psychologically/emotionally driven while others are strategically sensitive. Others have a faster grasp of new business trends while others are not. Also stakeholders, opinion leaders and media houses, may present differing views about CSR thus posing a further challenge. To avoid these boardroom challenges The most important guiding factor is to strike a balance between the company goals and the specific agenda of the board and its members. Seeking some independent opinion on matters that seem unclear will always guide the board or top management in reaching a strategic and well informed CSR involvement decision.

grate and maximize available resources within the internal and external environment for the attainment of organizational or societal goals (Ogbonnia, 2007).

From the definitions above, we can observe that leadership becomes a crucial element if a company wants to be involved in CSR. There is need for a direction and a person behind the "CSR initiatives." For example, some companies have branded themselves as, "we are the leaders in CSR, cited from Aga Khan," and "no one knows more in CSR than we do," as well as "we are the leading CSR information and advisory source" (cited from www.uccsri.com), and "our vision is to be the benchmarks in CSR" (cited from the CSR Consultative Group, at www.csrconsultativegroup.com), etc. This means that getting involved in CSR is much more than just observing a simple match. It involves incorporating the capacity to provide direction and motivation, coupled with providing room for necessary innovations, as this is crucial.

Effective Corporate Societal Interface Management requires effective leadership, making a trade-off between more or less managerial control and ability of individuals to influence a group to realize a given objective. Leadership ensures that people want to do things and are good managers (Van and Van (2006). CSR can be regarded as an on-going and strategic process, where different actors within and outside the company are involved. To ensure successful involvement in CSR throughout the company, it is vital to have leaders (boardroom members) serve as active proponents of CSR. According to Van and Van (2006), there are four major types of CSR Approaches and Leadership. These include: In-active, Re-active, Active, and Pro/Interactive.

i. In-active Transactional and Team Leaders' Approach: Here, 'Transactional' and 'Team' leaders are particularly good at specifying in-active and re-active CSR goals, clarifying roles and responsibilities, and motivating their subordinates to achieve group or organizational goals (ibid). These leaders display a strong similarity to 'ordinary' managers, focusing largely on internal operations of the company/organization. Transactional leadership is by nature primarily efficiency oriented, and these leaders will be primarily interested in corporate self-interest.

ii. Re-active Charismatic Leaders' Approach: This approach will focus primarily on internal operations of the organization, and will display an ability to present a vision of the future of the organization in combination with strong personal commitment and strong character. These leaders appeal to the idea of "trust me" in their rapport with employees. However, it is difficult for others to emulate their leading personal traits. Charismatic leaders in this approach, in the view of employees, show a great deal of responsiveness to the needs of employees and, in case of CSR, to society.

iii. Active-Visionary and Moral Leaders' Approach: This is approach is characterized by a more active stance on CSR. Both the leaders and the followers require an idea/vision of where the organization should be in the future. They derive their legitimacy, in particular, from ethical principles on which their vision is based. They focus on communicating their vision to stakeholders inside as well as outside the organization. They are strongly goal oriented, but regularly lack the practical orientation to link goals and vision to implementation. The visionary and moral leaders can be considered a pre-condition for "transformational leadership" (e.g., the Pro/Inter-active approach).

iv. Pro/Inter-Active Transformational Leaders' Approach: This is the most outwardly oriented type of leadership. It is directed at formulating and implementing a new organizational vision that is embedded in a broader vision of society and the active involvement of external stakeholders.

Table 4   CSR and Its Future for Organizational Involvement

CSR is a concept whereby organizations consider the interests of society by taking responsibility of customers, suppliers, employees, shareholders, communities and other stakeholders as well, to analyze capability availability and the long-term effects of climatic change, reduction of carbon emissions, energy conservation and supply chain sustainability. CSR holds organizations considering the overall interests of society of its day to day business. The future of CSR centers on aspects like role of business, changes in regulatory frameworks and social trends.

2.5 CSR DIMENSIONS AVAILABLE FOR COMPANIES' INVOLVEMENT

There are various options available through which companies may become involved in CSR. These can be referred to as CSR Dimensions. Although different scholars like Carroll (1979; 1999), Nkiko (2009), Katamba and Gisch-Boie (2008) and Visser (2008; 2009) will present to you different dimensions, it is important to recognize that they draw these dimensions based upon their perceptions and definition of CSR. The CSR definition that we adopted in this book, *Principles of CSR,* has some traces of a stakeholder orientation. Hence, based on the stakeholder theory by Freeman and Philip (2002), (already discussed in Chapter One), we see that CSR has the following main dimensions: Workplace, marketplace, community, and environment.

The company will consider what dimensions/options, or combinations of them, are best for it and the fitness of the option to its past and current operations. A good rule of thumb is that customers, employees, local community and local press will be interested to learn about the initiatives your company takes that show commitment to corporate social responsibility. We provide a CSR matrix below to provide an insight into the CSR dimensions, the stakeholders, as well as the likely benefits accruing from each CSR dimension (see Table 5 and Table 6).

Each CSR dimension has a representative "audience" of stakeholders. Developing a successful CSR program and sustainable strategies requires a careful analysis of the various audiences involved. These include:

Table 5   CSR Matrix

CSR Dimension	Workplace	Market	Community	Environment	Governance
Stakeholders	• Employees and their families • Unions • Local community	• Consumers • Consumer groups • Suppliers • Competitors	• Local community • Nongovernmental organization • Schools	• Environmental organizations • Consumers • Business partners	• Public & private sector • All business partners • Government
Areas of involvement (where CSR enters a company)	• Remuneration • Work-life balance • Training • Health	• Product quality, product security • Fair price • Fairbusiness partnership	• Sponsoring of events, etc. • Activities of employees • Donations	• Save energy and costs • Renewable energy • Environmental impacts at the project site	• Internal company structures • Transparency • Accountability • Succession planning
Benefits to the company	• Less sick leaves • Higher motivation • Less turnover	• More customer satisfaction • Improved production process • New products	• Better reputation • License to operate • Higher Identification of employees	• Less energy and costs • Improved Image and innovation	• Better reputation • Better profitability and sustainability

Source: Adopted from the strategic plan of the CSR Consultative Group of Uganda (used with permission). For details about the group, please visit www.csrconsultativegroup.com.

Table 6   Audiences to CSR Dimensions

It is very important to note that each CSR dimension has a target audience/stakeholders. Let us briefly have a look at them:

- **Marketplace Audiences:** If a company wants to raise awareness about the way it operates responsibly in the market, it will opt to talk to employees, customers, consumer associations, suppliers, business partners and investors of that marketplace.
- **Work Place Audience:** If a company wants to make a statement about improvements in work place policies, it will be guided to inform employees, trade unions (if any are involved), the local community, and the public authorities about the changes.
- **Environment Audiences:** If a company wants to communicate about its CSR initiatives that can help to preserve the environment, it will consider talking to employees, business partners, relevant not-for-profit organizations, consumers, public authorities and the community at large. For example, tourist organizations can communicate the initiatives that put the environment first to their customers, employees, and others. A good example from Europe is the Eco-label system and its benefits to tourists, employees, and the organizations themselves. Freeman and Philip (2002) argue that a company will not pollute air for the sake of profit because the company will also consider the interest of people living in the locality.
- **Community Audience:** If a company wants to convey CSR initiatives about its commitment to the local community, it should focus on employees, relevant local organizations or institutions (such as schools, hospitals and associations), public authorities and relevant not-for-profit organizations.

2.6 CONCLUSION

Organizations need to embrace CSR because the chances are high that it will improve their environment by making them continuously behave in a way that ultimately contributes to their own economic development even while improving the quality of life for all of the audiences involved with them. Getting involved in CSR brings positive outcomes focusing on economic, social and environmental goals with longer term perspectives. However, as a new concept, there is a need to create more awareness about how organizations can get involved and more so communicating its potential benefits, the possible challenges, and the different approaches these organizations can employ.

2.7 LEARNING ASSIGNMENTS

1. Study an organization of your choice and try to establish what social responsibilities it has been, or is, or is not at all engaged in. Consider how this organization makes its CSR strategic decisions. Determine whether or not the organization provides individuals with any guidelines to help with decision-making, and whether or not it allows them to make their own decisions. Establish if the company's CSR status could be improved.

2. a) Look at the objectives of "your" chosen organization and obtain performance reports for the organization before it began engaging CSR and after. Specifically evaluate and compare before-and-after performance in each of the following: profitability, efficiency, growth, shareholder return, resource utilization, reputation, market leadership/share, technological leadership and survival.
   b) Review the organization's governance to evaluate its CSR levels. Draw appropriate conclusions after concluding the review. You will then be in a position to confirm or refute any claims made by "your" organization.
   c) Make an analysis of all the company's resources throughout the company's value chain, and establish the difference in growth, stagnation, or reduction of various resources and the competitive advantage realized.

2.8 REFERENCES

Balou, B., Heiteger, D. L., and Landesm C. (2006). The Future of Corporate Sustainability Reporting. *Journal of Accounting.* Vol. 202 (6), pp. 65–74.

Baron D. B. (2001). Private Politics, CSR and Integrated Strategy. *Journal of Economics and Management Strategy.* Vol. 10, No. 1, pp. 7–45.

Bath Consultancy Group (no date). *CSR-Milton Friedman Was Right.* http://www.bathconsultancygroup.com/documents/CSR%20-

%20Milton%20Friedman%20was%20right.pdf, retrieved on June 16, 2011.

Bhattacharya, C. B., Sanker, S., and Korschun, D. (2008). Using CSR to Win the War for Talent. *Management Review,* 49 (2), 37–44.

Carroll, A. B. (1990). Corporate Social Responsibility: Evolution of a Definitional Construct. *Business and Society,* 38 (3), 268–295.

Day, G. S. and Nedungad, P. (1994). Managerial representations of competitive advantage. *Journal of Marketing,* 58 (4), 31–44.

Freeman, R. E. and Philip, R. A. (2002). Stakeholder Theory: A Libertarian Defense. *Business Ethics Quarterly,* Vol. 12, No. 3, 33.

Friedman, M. (1970). "The Social Responsibility of Business Is to Increase Its Profits." *The New York Times Magazine* (13th Sept), 32–33, 122–126.

Girod, S. and Michael, B. (2003). "Branding in European Retailing: A Corporate Social Responsibility Perspective." *European Retail Digest,* Vol. 38, 1–6.

Katamba, D. and Gish-Boie, S. (2008). *CSR in Uganda: Perceptions, Approaches and Needs of Companies.* http://www.livinge-arth.org.uk/africa_programmes/uganda/CSR_study.pdf. Accessed 20th January, 2009.

Kouzes, J. and Posner, B. (2007). *The Leadership Challenge.* CA: Jossey Bass.

Levine, M. A. (August 13, 2008). The Benefits of Corporate Social Responsibility (Electronic version). New York Law Journal online, August 13, 2008. Retrieved June 16, 2011 from http://www.law.com/jsp/ihc/PubArticleIHC. jsp?id= 1202423730339

Levis, J. (2005). "Adoption of Corporate Social Responsibility Codes by Multinational Companies." http://www. Sciencedirect.com/Science Article (accessed November 2010).

Loe, T. W., Ferrell, L., and Mansfield, P. (2000). Review of empirical studies assessing ethical decision making in business: *A journal of business ethics,* Vol. 25 (3), 185–204.

Mittal, R. K., Sinha, N., and Singh, A. (2008). An Analysis of Linkage between Economic value added and Corporate Social Responsibility. *Management Decision.* Vol. 46 (9), 1437–1443.

Norris, G. and O'Dwyer, B. (2004). Motivating socially responsive decision making: the operation of management controls in a social responsive organization. *British Accounting Review,* Vol. 36 (2), 173–96.

Ogbonnia, K. S. (2007). *Political party system and effective leadership in Nigeria: A contingency approach.* Dissertation. Walden University, 2007, p. 27.

Pava, L. and Krauz, J. (1996). The Association between Corporate Social Responsibility and Financial Performance. *Journal of Business Ethics.* 15, 132–57.

Preston, L. and O'Bannon, D. (1997). The Corporate Social-Financial Performance Relationship. *Business and Society Journal.* 36, 5–31.

Stigliz, J. (2008). *The Current Financial Challenges: Policy and Regulatory Implications.* Conference for the 27th International CIRIEC Conference. Seville, Spain.Terje I. Vaaland and Morten Heide (2008), "Managing corporate social responsibility: lessons from the oil industry," Corporate Communications: An International Journal, Volume 13, No. 2, pp. 212–225 Van, T, R. and Van, D.Z. (2006). *International Business society Management: Linking Responsibility and globalization.* London. New York: Routledge.

Visser, W. (2008). Corporate Social Responsibility (CSR) in Developing Countries. In: Crane, A., Matten, D., McWilliams, A., Moon, J., Siegel, D. (Eds.) *The Oxford Handbook Of Corporate Social Responsibility,* New York, Oxford University Press.

Wheelen,T. and Hunger J. D. (2006), *Cases in Strategic Management and Business Policy.* Upper Saddle River, NJ: Pearson Prentice Hall.

3

Integrating Corporate Social Responsibility into Organizational Culture and Making It a Business Strategy

Isaac Newton Kayongo and Samuel Musigire

3.1 INTRODUCTION

This chapter highlights the concept of organizational culture and its relationship with Corporate Social Responsibility. It explains how Corporate Social Responsibility can be integrated in organizational culture and be made a business strategy.

CHAPTER OBJECTIVES AND LEARNING OUTCOMES:

At the end of this chapter students should understand:

1. The concept of organizational culture and its relationship with corporate social responsibility
2. The principles guiding the integration of CSR into organizational culture, and be able to use them effectively
3. How to design a business strategy with CSR as one of its components or to advocate the inclusion of CSR in any business strategy
4. How to guide the implementation of a CSR program, both within a specific organization and outside the organization

LIST OF SUB TOPICS INCLUDED IN THIS CHAPTER:

1. Definitions of organizational culture and Corporate Social Responsibility
2. Components of organizational culture
3. Principles that guide the integration of Corporate Social Responsibility into organizational culture, making it a business strategy.
4. Attributes of good CSR initiative and strategy
5. Using CSR as a competitive advantage tool

3.2 DEFINITION OF ORGANIZATIONAL CULTURE

Various authors have given definitions of organizational culture which are not very far apart. McShane (1988) defines organizational culture as, "The basic pattern of shared values and assumptions governing the way employees within an organization think about and act on problems and opportunities." Yet (Cameron & Ettington, 1988), while discussing organizational culture, observes that it includes "Dominant values that the organization advocates and expects participants to share." These encompass concepts such as high product and service quality, low absenteeism, and high efficiency. Similarly corporate social responsibility has been defined as the relationship between a corporation and its stakeholders, on one dimension, and the relationship between the corporation and the local community in which it resides (Aras and Crowther, 2009). It is also argued that the relationship should be well defined in the corporation's strategy and it should form part of its core values of the organizational culture.

In this respect Corporate Responsibility can be viewed and should be cultivated as part of the organizational culture, which should compliment and reflect the dominant values of the organization. Furthermore, the organization should ensure that organizational members share this as a deliverable to their customers, workers and other members of the general community. Once CSR has been accepted as part of the core values of the organization then budgeted resources should be committed to that endeavor.

Aligning CSR Definition with Organizational Culture

The World Business Council for Sustainable Development, in its publication "*Making Good Business Sense*," which was authored by Lord Holme and Richard Watts (January 2000), defined corporate social responsibility as follows:

"Corporate Social Responsibility is the continuing commitment by business to behave ethically and contribute to economic development while improving the quality of life of the workforce and their families as well as of the local community and the general society at large."

The European Community Defines Corporate Social Responsibility As:

"A concept whereby companies decide voluntarily to contribute to a better society and to a cleaner environment. It is a concept whereby companies integrate social and environmental concerns in their business operations and interaction with their stakeholders on a voluntary basis."

In 2009, while compiling his 'Questions and Answers' regarding *'corporate social responsibility in the downturn,'* Martha Lagace[1] interviewed Prof. V. Kasturi Rangan.[2] The professor defined Corporate Social Responsibility (CSR) as "activities undertaken by businesses that enhance their value in the community and society and thus benefit their reputation and brand. In general these activities create a win-win for the company and its larger group of stakeholders." From this feedback, we see that CSR should be treated as a business discipline and practiced with the same professionalism and rigor as other aspects of a firm's strategy (which the concept of organizational culture emphasizes).

Also what emerges from the above definitions and discussions is that CSR has to do with the concerns of both the internal stakeholders and external stakeholders. The internal stakeholders will include, among others, the workforce, and the external will include the community at large and the pertinent environmental concerns. A company is expected to be socially responsible, thus it must have programs to better the working conditions of its workers, serve the interests of the general public (especially in the area where it is located), and to take care of the immediate environment. This may be accomplished by, for instance, avoiding polluting the physical/natural environment and the destruction of the surrounding eco system.

---

[1] Senior editor of *HBS Working Knowledge*

[2] The Malcolm P. McNair Professor of Marketing at Harvard Business School. He is also a co chair of the Social Enterprise Initiative (with Herman B. "Dutch" Leonard) as well as faculty chair of the Executive Education program Corporate Social Responsibility

3.3 COMPONENTS OF ORGANIZATIONAL CULTURE

There are four types of organizational culture which were identified by Quinn and Rorbaugh (1983) in their *'The competing Values Map.'* The recent (2009) works of Ülle Übius, Ruth Alas at Estonian Business School, *'Organizational Culture Types as Predictors of Corporate Social Responsibility'* Seem to have substantiated these organizational culture issues by specifically relating them to CSR. These scholars' ideas, combined with other scholars,' are identified and discussed as follows:

(A) A HIERARCHICAL CULTURE

A hierarchical structure is one of the seven characteristics of a classic bureaucracy, as outlined by Max Weber. Cameron and Quinn (1999) also identified hierarchy as one of the more dominant features of organizational culture. A hierarchical culture results in a highly formalized and structured place to work. Formal rules and policies which come from above hold the organization together. The hierarchical culture promotes the long-term concerns of the organization which include stability, predictability and efficiency.

(B) THE MARKET CULTURE

The Market Culture is based on the assumption that the external environment is "not benign but hostile." Hence an organization must be keen on external positioning and control. The organization must address and properly handle its relationships with external stakeholders/constituencies including suppliers, customers, contractors, licensees, unions, and regulators. The organization which emphasizes the above values will achieve competitiveness and productivity, which is the ultimate goal of any organization (Cameron & Ettington, 1988).

(C) THE CLAN CULTURE

Firms with a dominant "clan culture" emphasize teamwork, employee involvement, support programs, and corporate commitment to employees. Some basic assumptions in this culture are that the environment can best be managed through teamwork and employee development, customers are best thought of as partners, and the organization is in the business of developing a humane work environment. The clan culture is said to be held together by loyalty and tradition. The organization considers cohesion and morale to be the long-term benefit which emanates from the optimal development of each individual employee (Cameron 1998).

(D) THE ADHOCRACY CULTURE

According to Cameron and Quinn (1999), "a major goal of an adhocracy is to foster adaptability; flexibility and creativity where uncertainty, ambiguity, and/or information overload are typical. An important challenge of these organizations is to produce innovative products and services and to adapt quickly to new opportunities. A high emphasis on individuality, risk taking and anticipating the future exists as almost everyone in an adhocracy becomes involved with production, clients, research and development and so forth."

Principles for Integrating CSR into Organizational Culture

Basically, three principles of CSR have been identified and these can be used to integrate CSR into an organizational culture. These principles include Sustainability, Accountability, and Transparency, and many organizations consider these principles as part of their core values.

a. **Sustainability**: Sustainability refers to the ability of the corporation to continue sustaining its operations given the scarcity of resources. Some corporations use resources in their processes, especially the natural resources which can become depleted and make it difficult to sustain the operations. In such cases, corporations are urged to use resources sparingly and engage in practices which are designed to renew the source base, such as the planting of trees and forests. Where possible, such businesses should prioritize their renewable resources. Some corporations have to spend more money on research and development to finding methods of conserving and developing alternative sources. One example is an organization with a CSR fund where employees are convinced and willing contribute to it, or where the organization recruits partners who contribute resources that the particular organization cannot raise independently. The endeavor must remain a lifetime policy if the organization is to survive over the long term.

b. **Accountability**: Accountability is concerned with the recognition that the company's actions affect the external environment. Thus it should act responsibly (i.e., that it should engage in activities which are environmentally friendly). It is supposed to report to stakeholders those actions which have a potential to affect the environment, and the actions proposed to mitigate or to minimize such impacts. In many countries, national governments have enacted laws designed to ensure the well being of the environment. In Uganda the government enacted an environment statute through which the National Environment Management Authority was created. This is a national body which regulates and approves projects after ensuring that they are either environmentally friendly or that mitigation measures are incorporated in the project designs.

c. **Transparency**: The Transparency principle, in the context of corporate social responsibility, means that "the external impact of the actions of the organization can be ascertained from that organization's reporting and pertinent facts are not disguised within that reporting" (Crowther and Aras, 2008). Business or management must be aware that all stakeholders, including those external to the organization, are entitled to know through reports all the effects of the organizations acts and transactions, especially as it affects them and the environment. For example, external stakeholders will want to know what the business has done to mitigate adverse impacts from its operations. This requires the timely filing if impact reports, with any relevant shortcomings shown. This final principle naturally emanates from the other two. For instance, it clearly emanates from the accountability principle that management must realize an accountability to the general population for their actions.

From the preceding information the following conclusions can be reached:

i. CSR enhances the brand image and reputation of a business and also leads to improvement in sales and customer loyalty and increased ability to attract and retain employees (Sharma et al, 2009).

ii. It is necessary for practitioners within the various departments of an organization to support the integration of CSR throughout the business strategy and operations.

iii. CSR efforts will be successful to the degree that they are supported by a strong board and secure the chief executive officer's (CEO's) commitment.

iv. Marketing managers need to carry out internal marketing in their organizations. They can organize meetings and workshops for the board of directors/governing council and top managers through which they can be made aware and convinced that getting involved in CSR activities produces a good business image and improves sales for the organization.

Organizations ought to make CSR part of their core values. CSR should be integrated in corporate missions and codes of conduct. Organizations should educate employees and partners about the need to observe the above principles; rules and codes of conduct should be put in place and penalties for breaking them should be written and communicated to the concerned parties.

The stakeholders within organizations should target include employees, customers, communities, and society in general. CSR with employees may involve putting in place a policy for providing them with the appropriate tools and clothing for work.

3.4 DEVELOPING A SUITABLE CORPORATE SOCIAL RESPONSIBILITY STRATEGY FOR SOCIALLY AND ENVIRONMENTALLY RESPONSIBLE PRODUCTS AND SERVICES, WORKFORCE, AND COMMUNITY RELATIONS

Studies such as that conducted by Cornelius, Todres, Janjuha-Jivraj, Woods, & Wallace (2008), have found corporate social responsibility to be an integral part of the business vocabulary. It is regarded as a crucially important issue in management. Companies which aim to adhere to all universally accepted ethical standards of social behavior are in a position to expect a positive attitude and support in the modern society. Moreover, helping to solve burning social and ecological problems can help a company to secure competitive advantages, and thus ensure their success in the future (Juščius & Snieška, 2008).

The CSR model in the work of Carroll (1999), included four components: economic, legal, ethical and voluntary (discretionary). The economic aspect concerns itself with the economic performance of the company, while the other three categories address the social aspect of corporate social responsibility. Hillman and Kein (2001) and Baron (2001) also agree that stakeholder-oriented CSR is positively correlated with financial performance. This means that a company aiming at maximizing profits will certainly have to include the key economic component of CSR.

According to Susniene and Vanagas (2007), it is necessary to achieve a high level of stakeholder satisfaction, keeping in mind that the most important stakeholder group is the organization's customers. It follows that through satisfaction of their interests, other stakeholder interests can also be satisfied. Ruževičius, and Sarafinas (2007) observed that the image and reputation of organization in the social and environmental fields will affect consumers and customers more and more. This means that in order to attract more customers and consumers, CSR issues should take a focal position in strategy formulations.

Further studies have found the labor market to be very competitive, with qualified workers preferring to work for and stay at those companies that care about their employees. Similarly it has been found that there are tendencies for investors to invest in companies that practice and report CSR.

3.5 CORPORATE SOCIAL RESPONSIBILITY AS A TOOL FOR ACHIEVING A COMPETITIVE ADVANTAGE

CSR is one of the important ways in which an organization can distinguish itself from its competitors. The strategic CSR investor, upon making a social investment, may obtain the following advantages or benefits (for details, please revisit chapter two):

i. A superior reputation
ii. Differentiated products that extract a premium
iii. More highly qualified personnel, as many people are attracted to socially responsible organizations, thereby giving such organizations an opportunity to choose the best people out of the many who are available
iv. The above factors all lead to greater profits

CSR designs may involve either the position of the firm with respect to its competitors or the leveraging of distinctive resources and competences. Both society and firms are better off when firms use CSR strategically than when they are coerced into making such investments. Javis (2009) states that CSR has to be "remarkable" and then proceeds to highlight what makes for remarkable CSR:

   i. *Publicity*—an organization which breaks ranks within its industry knows that things have to change, even while everyone has been holding on hoping things were yet to change

  ii. *Sustainability*—taking the time required to understand what true sustainability would look like, and then proceeding to achieve sustainability in the company and announcing this vision as your target

 iii. *CSR Planning*—designing a clear plan that outlines how to get where the company where it must be going

 iv. *Selling*—sharing the imperatives with involved shareholders, and standing up to those who think it is fine so long as it does not affect next quarter's profits

  v. *Understanding*—recognizing that your customers are also citizens, not just consumers, and reflecting that in the products you make and the marketing you do.

 vi. *Lobbying*—approaching governments when you see market signals that will promote socially undesirable outcomes, even if they may benefit you in the short term

3.6 Conclusion

From the above discussion, it has been established that corporate social responsibility is a core value and it has been found to be an integral part of the organizational culture in performing firms. Its advantages include enhanced morale and commitment from staff, which will improve productivity on their part and compel the organization to recognize high performance. The development of individuals also interests them. Overall, CSR has been found to contribute to a positive image in the market place for the firms which practice it. Hence, since corporate social responsibility contributes to a good image for any company, and because it is also designed to increase performance, it is our conclusion that it should be integrated in all organizational strategies as a core value designed to significantly contribute to taking the organization to where it wants to be.

3.7 SELF-TEST QUESTIONS

1. What is organizational culture?
2. What are the corporate social responsibility principles?
3. What is the relationship between corporate social responsibility and a competitive advantage for an organization?

3.8 REFERENCES

Alas, R. and Sun, W. (2008). Institutional impact of work-related values in Chinese organizations, *Journal of Business Ethics.* Vol. 83, No. 2, pp. 297–306.

Alas, R., Ennulo, J. and Türnpuu, L. (2006). Managerial values in the institutional context, *Journal of Business Ethics,* Vol. 65, No. 3, pp. 269–278.

Aras, G. and Crowther, D. (2009). *The durable corporation: Strategies for sustainable development.* Farnham, England: Gower.

Balmer J., Fukukawa K., and Gray A., (2007). The Nature and Management of Ethical Corporate Identity: A Commentary on Corporate Identity, Corporate Social Responsibility and Ethics, Journal of Business Ethics, Vol. 76, No.1, pp. 7–15.

Cameron, K. S. and Quinn, R. E. (1999). *Diagnosing and Changing Organizational Culture: Based on the Competing Values Framework.* Addison Wesley Longman, Reading, MA.

Cameron, K. S. and Ettington, D. R. (1988). The conceptual foundations of organizational culture, Higher Education: Handbook of Theory and Research, New York: Agathon, pp. 356–396.

Carroll, A. B. (1999). Corporate social responsibility: Evolution of a definitional construct, *Business & Society,* Vol. 38, No. 3, pp. 268–295.

Cornelius, N., Todres, M,. Janjuha-Jivraj, S., Woods, A., Wallace, J. (2008). Corporate Social Responsibility and the Social Enterprise. Journal of Business Ethics, Vol. 81, pp. 355–370.

Crowther, D. and Guler, A. (2008). *Corporate Social Responsibility.* David Crowther and Guler Aras & Ventus Publishing APS.

Dr. Carol Reader, International & Comparative Management San José State University.

Drucker, P. F. (1984). The new meaning of Corporate Social Responsibility, California Management Review, 26, pp. 53–63.

Hillman, A. and Keim, G. (2001). Shareholder value, stakeholder management, and social issues: what's the bottom line? Strategic Management Journal, Vol. 22, No. 2, pp. 125–139.

Juščius, V. and Snieška, V. (2008). Influence of Corporate Social Responsibility on Competitive Abilities of Corporations, Engineering Economics, Vol. 3, No. 58, pp. 34–44.

Marcel van Marrewijk (2003). Concepts and definitions of CSR and Corporate Sustainability: Between Agency and Communication. *Journal of Business Ethics,* 44, 2/3, pp. 95–105.

Quinn, R. E. and Rohrbaugh, J. (1983). A spatial model of effectiveness criteria: Towards a competing values approach to organizational analysis. *Management Science,* Vol. 29, pp. 363–377

Rangan Kasturi (2009). Corporate Social Responsibility in a Downturn (presentation in a seminar) Responsibility and Ethics, *Journal of Business Ethics,* 2007, 76, pp. 7–15.

Ruževičius, J. and Serafinas D. (2007). The Development of Socially Responsible Business in Lithuania, *Engineering Economics,* Vol. 1, No. 51, pp. 36–43.

Susnienė D. and Vanagas, P. (2007). Means for Satisfaction of Stakeholders' Needs and Interests, *Engineering Economics,* Vol. 5, No. 55, pp. 36–43.

4

Implementation, Tracking, (Measuring and Assessing) CSR Undertakings, and Managing CSR Communications

David Katamba, Charles Tushabomwe-Kazooba,
and Babiiha Mpisi Sulayman

4.1 INTRODUCTION

This chapter endeavors to offer guidelines for translating the CSR idea/decision into action. It includes recommendations for tracking (assessing) progress, and how to produce optimal CSR communications. These three areas have proved to be of great concern, especially if you are scheduled to present CSR ideas in the Boardroom for approval or to secure more resources to sustain the CSR agenda/undertaking from any concerned stakeholders. In case the idea of CSR is new in your organization, the chapter further prepares you for a key step: Implementation! It is important to note that the chapter has been kept small in scope due to the nature and level of understanding required for the reader. That is, this text is intended to introduce the reader to the basic principles of CSR, as opposed to offering an overwhelming amount of more complex information. For more detailed reading and understanding, various cross referencing has been provided.

At the end of this chapter the reader should be able to:

1. List the appropriate CSR performance and tracking tools for CSR undertakings
2. Profile audiences/stakeholders for different CSR communications
3. List performance indicators for ongoing/planned CSR activities
4. Profile and report on CSR accomplishments based on acceptable tools
5. Separate CSR communications from Public relations and Marketing campaigns
6. Design and use simple CSR implementation, monitoring and evaluation tools
7. Write CSR reports and Design CSR communication messages

SUB-TOPICS COVERED IN THIS CHAPTER ARE:

1. Implementation of CSR
2. Tracking (Assessing and Measuring)
3. CSR Performance
4. CSR Communications

4.2 IMPLEMENTATION OF CSR UNDERTAKINGS AND DECISIONS

According to Industry Canada (http://www.ic.gc.ca/eic/site/csr-rse.nsf/eng/rs00135.html), CSR Implementation refers to "the day-to-day decisions, processes, practices and activities that ensure the firm meets the spirit and letter of its CSR commitments and thereby carries out its CSR strategy." It further points out that, "If CSR commitments can be called 'talking the walk,' then implementation is 'walking the talk.'" Or simply put it, "Implementing the CSR strategy and commitments is all about translating talk into action—integrating the firm's CSR strategy and commitments into the daily routine." CSR implementation varies across industries. This means that there may be no "one size fits all" implementation model. However, various approaches exist in different economic settings as shown in Table 7.

In Uganda, the CSR Consultative Group has designed a tool kit to guide in the implementation of CSR across firms in Uganda and in similar developing economies. For details, visit: www.uccsri.com and www.csrconsultativegroup.com. A quick look through the tool kit shows that we may not easily find a uniform model for corporate

Table 7   The Core Research Article for Designing and Implementing Corporate Social

---

François Maon, Adam Lindgreen, and Valérie Swaen, (2009), Designing and Implementing Corporate Social Responsibility: An Integrative Framework Grounded in Theory and Practice, *Journal of Business Ethics*, Volume 87, Supplement 1/April 2009.

About the article:
Though conducted in Switzerland context, the article introduces an integrative framework of corporate social responsibility (CSR) design and implementation. It begins with a review of CSR literature relating particularly to design and implementation models. It also provides the background to develop a multiple case study. It further shows an integrative framework, based on multiple case studies and Lewin's change model, the four stages that span the nine steps of the CSR design and implementation process. It concludes with identifying and highlighting to the reader the various critical success factors for the CSR implementation process.

---

social responsibility implementation. This is because different economies, businesses and industries are at different levels of corporate social responsibility knowledge and development. Also, a detailed look at the tool kit (pp. 13–19) gives an impression that CSR implementation is not an event, but rather a process. This agrees with what the Government of Canada, through its publication, "CSR: An Implementation Guide for Canadian Business," page 19, suggests. Hence, the tool kit provides the following steps as soft stages to ensure successful CSR implementation:

1. Assess the current corporate social responsibility position and define aspirations: In this stage, a quick (Strengths, Weaknesses, Opportunities, and Threats) (SWOT) analysis is necessary so as to determine where the firm's strength lays. Thereafter, the company should develop its aspirations concerning corporate social responsibility strategy by finding answers to the following strategic questions:

    i. What is the company's overall aspiration in the market?

    ii. How important is corporate social responsibility in achieving this aspiration?

    iii. Who are the key stakeholder groups (government, consumers, NGOs, employees, etc.)?

2. What should be the company's specific corporate social responsibility goal (objective, timing, etc.)? Prioritize corporate social responsibility options issues/themes: With the help of the knowledge of Value Chain and corporate social responsibility funnel analyses, select the best CSR option(s) to engage in.

3. Define and design core elements of the corporate social responsibility program: Here, in light of the corporate social responsibility Options in (2) above, proceed to make decisions by examining its conciseness and consistence with the business agenda/strategy. Decisions made may relate to:

    i. Target market (employees, suppliers, out-of-school youths, etc.)

    ii. Geographical scope of the intended activity

    iii. Operational involvement

    iv. Partners to be involved

    v. Experience required

    vi. Communication style (should we use memo, meetings, media agencies, etc.)

4. Build the corporate social responsibility business case: This is when we make the corporate social responsibility idea/undertaking more realistic (cost verses revenue analysis) so as to present and defend it in the Boardroom (already discussed in Chapter Two). This is mainly aided by highlighting, among others, the following key issues:

    a. Time frame: Clarify both the short-term immediate objectives and the long-term goals and benefits.

    b. Nature of benefits: Identify the benefits accruing from such a corporate social responsibility undertaking/proposal. Benefits may be tangible (e.g., revenue from gaining access to new markets), or intangible (e.g., enhanced community goodwill, reputation, and/or employee morale).

    c. Benefit split: Justify how benefits are to be shared between internal and external stakeholders (e.g., the business and society). If they are one-sided, especially societal, it may be that you are moving into philanthropy and not strategic corporate social responsibility. Remember strategic corporate social responsibility is always about a win-win situation.

5. Ensure successful implementation of the corporate social responsibility program through monitoring and evaluation, or through

any scientific and managerial means. Along with other models and tools, a balanced score card (discussed later in this chapter) may be a useful tool to guide you through this stage.

In addition to the core research article of this section and the CSR Consultative Group's training tool kit, we can also borrow from "CSR: An Implementation Guide for Canadian Business," which suggested the sub-steps to ensure successful implementation of corporate social responsibility Options/commitments (Table 8).

Table 8   Steps to Ensure CSR Implementation:

1. Develop an integrated CSR decision-making structure
2. Prepare and implement a CSR business plan
3. Set measurable targets and identify performance measures
4. Engage employees and others to whom CSR commitments apply
5. Design and conduct CSR training
6. Establish mechanisms for addressing problematic behavior
7. Create internal and external communications plans

For details about these steps, please visit the site:
http://www.ic.gc.ca/eic/site/csr-rse.nsf/eng/rs00135.html

Source: *"CSR: An Implementation Guide for Canadian Business"* pp. 49–56.

The extract in Figure 1 (following page), is a flowchart from CRH, an international leader in the building materials industry. It shows how CSR is implemented at this company. That is, it shows and explains "how they apply (implement) CSR concepts in the daily management of their corporate governance, environment, health & safety and social activities." These four areas encompass all that is germane to the scope of this company's CSR performance and reporting, and reflect the interests of all its stakeholders.

4.3 TRACKING, MEASURING AND ASSESSING CSR UNDERTAKINGS

4.3.1 Process for Tracking, Measuring and Assessing Corporate Social Responsibility Undertakings

Corporate social responsibility tracking may synonymously be referred to as CSR Monitoring and Evaluation (M&E). Borrowing

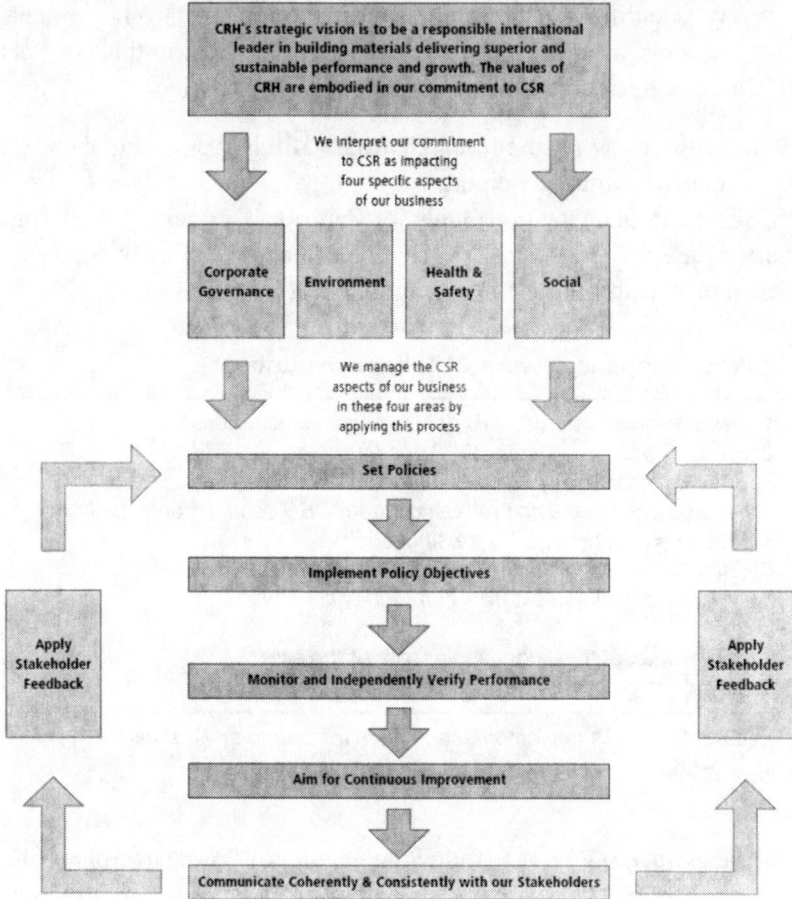

Figure 1—CSR Implementation Guide at CRH

from the GTZ BACKUP Initiative's M&E Tool kit (GTZ, 2007), we learn that Monitoring is "the routine tracking of aspects of programme or project performance, through record-keeping, reporting and surveillance, …facility observation and client surveys." The kit also highlights that Evaluation is "an episodic assessment of overall achievements; it attempts to link a particular output or outcome directly to an intervention after a period of time."

Therefore, if we are guided by this understanding of "M& E" we see that monitoring is a "during-process" activity while Evaluation is an "after or end-process" activity. We can therefore state that CSR Monitoring and Evaluation (M&E) is a process used to gather and provide data on CSR activity, progress and effectiveness, so as to allow for accountability to management and stakeholders. CSR M&E also provides data to ascertain and plan for future resource needs, and it also provides data useful for policy-making and advocacy. In addition, M&E of CSR activities provides government officials, development managers, and civil society with a better means for learning from past experience, improving service delivery, planning and allocating resources, and demonstrating results as part of accountability to stakeholders.

Monitoring and evaluation (M & E) of corporate social responsibility activities and undertaking can take form of:

i. Internal monitoring and evaluation. This is M&E conducted by local or regional company personnel or headquarters personnel, or a combination of employees from each group. Mostly importantly, an internal M&E person must be part of the company being monitored and evaluated.

ii. External Monitoring. This is M&E that involves the use of an outside agent or agency to monitor and evaluate company compliance with its set corporate social responsibility initiatives or signed principles (e.g., if the company had signed up for UN Global Compact membership or GRI). This is usually conducted with ongoing consultation from the company being evaluated.

iii. Independent (third-party) Monitoring and evaluation. This occurs when the M&E system is entirely independent of the company being monitored/evaluated, and wherein a third-party assesses a firm's compliance with its corporate social responsibility undertakings. Usually, when a corporate social responsibility communication is publicly released, different stakeholders will take interest and may start following the company without formal notice, and they may even start monitoring and evaluating it very early on. At one point, or at periodic points and intervals, the evaluators may issue independent reports about a given industry. Thus, one should not be surprised to find their company included among others being actively assessed!

Corporate social responsibility measuring may be referred to as the process of quantifying any CSR activity, process, input, or anything else that is quantifiable so as to report about its performance, the extent of its occurrence, the impact created and/or its magnitude or trend. This measuring may be either qualitative or quantitative. In some disciplines, units of measurement are set either scientifically or mechanically. For example meters for distance, seconds for time, etc. These provide a benchmark as well as a unit of analysis after measuring outcomes (performance, extent, impact, magnitude, etc).

While different universal measurement units are already set in some disciplines (for example, seconds for time), there has been no universally agreed upon standard measure for corporate social responsibility. Various indices, tools and models (for example, the Balanced Score Card (BSC), the Environmental audit, the FTSE4Good Index, the GRI Guidelines, the UN Global Compact's 10 principles, the AA1000, etc) have been developed by different international bodies, academicians, management gurus, and schools of thoughts to assist in measuring corporate social responsibility. The emergence of numerous different tools provides clear evidence that there is no universally agreed upon measure of corporate social responsibility efficacy (Katamba and Gisch-Boie, 2008). However, different corporate social responsibility measuring tools are valid in different settings, and companies have made use of them in various contexts. The proceeding section examines a few of the tools used to measure corporate social responsibility.

4.3.2 Tools and Indices for Tracking, Measuring and Assessing CSR Undertakings

In this section, the reader should critically examine the differences in each tool and ascertain when it makes sense to use one certain tool instead of another tool. For instance, the FTSE4Good Index mainly concentrates on investors and gives a good overview for external stakeholders. The BSC takes the management perspective and supports strategic planning and management. GRI Guidelines and indicators help to structure CSR reports and communication, and may also serve as a tool for strategic planning, and so on.

To date, there are no universally accepted M&E standards or measuring tools for corporate social responsibility undertakings. Various international bodies suggest different tools. For example, the World Business Council for Sustainable Development (WBCSD) suggests usage of "Measuring Impact Framework (MIF)," while the Global Reporting Initiative (GRI) provides a number of other guidelines. The UN Global Compact also has a series of M&E frameworks, but they rotate around its ten guiding (10) principles. The same occurs with AccountAbility (AA) 1000, and other oversight bodies.

A few of these tools are highlighted below. Most importantly, however, we conclude by providing the reader with a simple template by which to conduct tracking (monitoring and evaluation) and otherwise measure and follow the company's corporate social responsibility undertakings. Regardless of the emergence of a variety of corporate social responsibility measurement tools, it is most important to know why we should endeavor to measure CSR undertakings correctly. Primarily, this enables us to know the exact contribution of corporate social responsibility (CSR) activities to a company as well as to its stakeholders (Panayiotou, Aravossis and Moschou, 2009).

Deciding Which Tool or Index to Use When Tracking, Measuring, and Assessing Corporate Social Responsibility Undertakings

Although there is currently no universal corporate social responsibility measurement tool, it is very important to remember that measurement of CSR takes into account both financial and non-financial aspects. Hence, a good corporate social responsibility measurement tool must have the capacity to investigate both aspects. A bias for one aspect over another may make the tool unacceptable, and distort any communication about CSR progress. In a bid to create more widely acceptable CSR measurement tools, we have brought a variety of them into use (as already highlighted above). Many of these tools were developed by accounting bodies (like GAAP, AA1000, etc), with measures which may be inclined more toward financial M&E than toward non-financial aspects. Other tools have been designed by UN environmental bodies such as UNEPI, as well as humanitarian bodies such as the UN Global Compact. Recent research (Katamba, 2010) has also revealed that one specific tool, CRITICS (Corporate Responsibility Index through Internet Consultation of Stakeholders), is gaining increasing acceptability. This tool was developed by MCH International, Ltd, (MCHi) in 1998 and it has twenty (20) questions that investigate and measure corporate social responsibility (For further details, visit http://www.mhcinternational.com).

Tools, CSR Checklists, Models, Frameworks, and Indices

Various tools and indices exist to measure corporate social responsibility. But due to the limited scope of this book we shall only look at a few of them, as shown in Table 9.

Table 9   Showing Some CSR measurement, Monitoring and Evaluation Tools and Indices

Tools	Balanced score card, The Natural step
Indices	FTSE4Good Index; SAM's Corporate Sustainability Assessment; Dow Jones Sustainability Index (DJSI); Sunday time great place to work; Corporate Health and safety performance index; Business in the community
Ethical rating agencies	EIRIS, Innovest, Asset4, Vigeo, and the ASPI index
Reporting institutes and registers	Global Reporting Initiatives (GRI), CERES, Institute for sustainability, and others

Source: Jo (2008).

FTSE4GOOD INDEX

The company's website explains that "The FTSE4Good Index Series has been designed to measure the performance of companies that meet globally recognized corporate responsibility standards, and to facilitate investment in those companies. Transparent management criteria alongside the FTSE brand make THE FTSE4Good the index of choice for the creation of Responsible Investment products."

Source: FTSE4Good Index website: http://www.ftse.com/

SAM'S CORPORATE SUSTAINABILITY ASSESSMENT

The company's website states that "SAM is an investment boutique focused exclusively on Sustainability Investing. The firm's offering comprises asset management indexes and private equity." To this end, it developed the tool, SAM's Corporate Sustainability Assessment. This tool is based on an extensive questionnaire. The questionnaire covers three dimensions—economic, environmental and social—and can be divided into general and industry specific criteria. SAM's approach goes beyond the conventional environmental, social and governance (ESG) framework and includes other intangible business issues that are critical to [a] company's long-term success, such as innovation management, customer relationship management, and brand management in consumer-driven industries. In other words, the questions address a broad range of issues of a long-term nature, which have an impact on corporate financial performance and are under-researched in traditional financial analysis.

Source: The sustainability Year book, 2010, p. 11, accessible online on: http://yearbooktool.sam-group.com/Download/Yearbook_2010.pdf

DOW JONES SUSTAINABILITY INDEX (DJSI)

The company's website states that "Dow Jones Indexes is a leading full-service index provider that develops, maintains and licenses indexes for use as benchmarks and as the basis of investment products. ...Launched in 1999, the Dow Jones Sustainability Indexes (DJSI) are the first global indexes tracking the financial performance of the leading sustainability-driven companies worldwide. They provide asset managers with reliable and objective benchmarks to manage sustainability portfolios. The DJSI follow a best-in-class approach and include sustainability leaders from each industry on a global and regional level, respectively. The annual review of the DJSI family is based on a thorough analysis of corporate economic, environmental and social performance, assessing issues such as corporate governance, risk management, branding, climate change mitigation, supply chain standards and labor practices. It accounts for general as well as industry specific sustainability criteria for each of the 57 sectors defined according to the Industry Classification Benchmark (ICB)."

Source: http://www.sustainability-index.com and www.dowjones.com

GLOBAL REPORTING INITIATIVE (GRI) GUIDELINES

The GRI Guidelines is an internationally recognized model for company CSR reports, and it seeks to develop globally standardized guidelines for sustainability reports. The GRI is primarily focused on major companies, but it is also used in connection with other ventures, such as organizations involved in environmental matters, human rights and labor issues, and by government agencies. The aim is to arrive at a comparable description of the economic, ecological and social contributions of the reporting entity. Application of GRI guidelines is voluntary and offers companies the opportunity to register on the GRI website (http://www.globalreporting.org/Home) (see Table 10).

Table 10   Point to Note

A GRI based CSR report may serve both as an internal tool for the company's CSR strategic planning as well as a communication tool toward the stakeholder.

ACCOUNTABILITY 1000 (AA1000)

AA1000 is a standard for social and ethical accounting, auditing and reporting. It assists companies in identifying indicators and goals with respect to their social consequences, gauging progress and reporting on what has been achieved.

For details, visit http://www.accountability21.net/

CRITICS

CRITICS is an acronym that stands for Corporate Responsibility Index through Internet Consultation of Stakeholders. With a few modifications, CRITICS may also be used to measure and investigate CSR. CRITICS are a subset of twenty questions that MHCi developed to assist in investigating companies/organizations in their quest to become more socially responsible. This framework of measurement was first developed in the USA by Prof. Donna Wood, who has so far applied it to dozens of companies to check its reliability and validity (see: The Planetary Bargain: CSR Matters, Earthscan, 2003).

ENVIRONMENTAL AUDIT

International Standards Organization (ISO), through its standard, ISO 14001, defines an environmental audit as, "the environmental standard against which organizations are assessed. It specifies the requirements for an Environment Management System (EMS), which provides a framework for an organization to control the environmental impacts of its activities, products and services."

According to the International Chamber of Commerce, an "environmental audit" is "the systematic examination of the interactions between any business operation and its surroundings. This includes all emissions to air, land, and water; legal constraints; the effects on the neighboring community, landscape and ecology; and the public's perception of the operating company in the local area. Environmental audit does not stop at compliance with legislation nor is it a 'greenwashing' public relations exercise. Rather it is a total strategic approach to the organization's activities." It is a systematic, objective and documented evaluation of the impact of the business activities on the environment.

(a) International Environmental Audit Guidelines and Bodies

(i) International Finance Corporation (IFC): The IFC is the private sector lending arm of the World Bank. As part of ensuring that the private sector companies participate in the development agenda, it (the IFC) developed an Environment Management System (EMS). The website of the Oil, Gas and Mining Sustainable Community Development Fund (CommDev) states that the EMS "is a practical tool that helps companies monitor and manage the impacts of their activities on the environment. It guides them on how to integrate environmental management into a company's daily operations, long-term planning and other management systems. The most important component of an EMS is an organizational commitment, based on a 'plan, do, check, and act' cycle, from the top of an organization to staff, to establish and refine environmental protection procedures that can be documented (and audited as required) to verify environmental performance to regulators and the community. To help small and medium-sized companies develop an EMS, the IFC Environment and Social Development Department has published a manual that outlines this structured approach to planning and implementing environment protection measures. Numerous government agencies, including the U.S. Environmental Protection Agency and Australia's Department of the Environment and Heritage, have endorsed the EMS concept." For details, visit: www.ifc.org

(ii) International Organization for Standardization (ISO). The website of the Oil, Gas and Mining Sustainable Community Development Fund (CommDev) state that the "ISO 14000 series is a collection of voluntary standards to help organizations meet the challenges of sustainable development" and CSR. The standards provide both a model for streamlining environmental management and guidelines to ensure that environmental issues are considered within a decision-making framework." The ISO website indicates that the "ISO has CD-ROM containing 20 published standards of the ISO 14000 family in a user-friendly configuration, along with related drafts nearing completion, including ISO 14040, which deals with the principles and requirements for conducting and reporting life-cycle assessment studies."

(b) Environmental Audit Guidelines and Bodies in Uganda

In Uganda, before a firm/company is granted a production license or investment license, an Environmental Impact Assessment (EIA) report has to be presented to the National Environment Management Authority (NEMA) and approved. This is a legal requirement by The National Environment Act Cap 153 and the National Environment (Waste Management) Regulations 1999. The EIA usually includes:

i. A description of the proposed project and, where applicable, of the reasonable alternative for its setting and design.

ii. A description of the environment likely to be affected.

iii. An assessment of the likely effects of the proposed project on the environment.

iv. A description of the measures proposed to eliminate, reduce or compensate for adverse environmental effects.

v. A distinction between the proposed and the existing environmental land use plan.

vi. An explanation of the reasons for the choice of the preferred site and project design rather than the alternative.

Non-compliance with the following (Table 11) by either a person or an organization could call for a legal action by NEMA.

THE BALANCED SCORE CARD (BSC)

Originally developed by Art Schneiderman (management process consultant at Analog Devices) in 1987, the BSC has been greatly improved by scholars and academicians, notably Robert Kaplan and David Norton in the year of 2000's. These scholars refer to BSC as "a strategic planning and management system used in business and industry, government, and non-profits worldwide to align business activities to the vision and strategy of the organization, improve internal and external communications and monitor organization performance against strategic goals." It focuses on measuring various overall performance indicators, often including customer perspective, internal-business processes, learning and growth and financials, in an attempt to monitor progress toward organization's strategic goals. Each major unit throughout the organization often establishes its own scorecard which, together with the scorecards of other units, is fundamental for the scorecard of the overall organiza-

Table 11   Legislation, Regulations and Guidelines on Environmental Auditing in Uganda

Uganda has a national environment policy and an environment sector 5-year plan/programme, reviewed every after 5 years. The National Environment Act, Cap. 153 established the NEMA as the principal agency in Uganda for the coordination, monitoring and supervision of all environmental matters. Under Section 53 of this Act, NEMA is mandated to make regulations and guidelines for the classification and management of hazardous wastes. NEMA released the following regulations and guidelines:

   i. The National Environment (Waste Management) Regulations 1999. These regulations apply to all categories of hazardous and non-hazardous waste; the storage and disposal of hazardous waste and their movement into and out of Uganda; and all waste disposal facilities, landfills, sanitary fills and incinerators;

  ii. The National Environment (Standards for Discharge of Effluent into Water or on Land) Regulations, 1999;

 iii. Environmental Audit Guidelines for Uganda, 1999;

 iv. Environmental Impact Assessment Regulations, 1998;

  v. Environmental Impact Assessment Guidelines,

 vi. Draft Environmental Oil Spillers Liability Regulations,

 vii. Draft Environmental Oil Spillers Liability Guidelines, and

viii. Draft Solid Waste Management Guidelines.

Source: *Compiled after literature review of the various legislations, regulations and guidelines on Environmental Auditing in Uganda, as indicated in the table above.*

tion. It was originally developed to measure non-financial aspects of a business. Currently, it has been refined to provide a balance in reporting both financial and non-financial aspects of business. Hence the modern revised BSC (Kaplan and Norton, 2000) has the following four dimensions: (1) Learning & growth: which includes training, learning, corporate culture and attitudes, self growth. (2) Business process: Metrics based on internal business processes which allow management to monitor how well the business is running and whether its products/services are well accepted by clients. (3) Customer: Indicators on customer satisfaction and tools to improve and monitor customer relations. Lastly (4) financial: where we look at operating income, return on capital employed in such corporate social responsibility undertakings, and notably the economic value/gain from such undertakings. Table 12 presents articles for core readings about the balanced score card.

Table 12   Articles for Core Readings about the Balanced Score Card (BSC)

Core Readings for this subtopic:

Aravossis, K., Panayiotou, N., & Tsousi, K. (2006), a proposed methodological framework for the evaluation of corporate social responsibility, in K. Aravossis, C. A. Brebbia, E. Kakaras, & A. G. Kungolos (Eds.), Environmental economics and investment assessment (pp. 87–95). Shouthampton, Boston: WIT Press.

Panayiotou Nikolaos A., Aravossis Konstantin G., and Moschou Peggy (2009), A New Methodology Approach for Measuring Corporate Social Responsibility Performance, *Water, Air, & Soil Pollution*: Focus, Volume 9, Numbers 1–2/April, 2009.

Brief about the articles:

They present innovative methods of performance measurements including the Balanced Scorecard which has been lately introduced in some companies in their attempt to include non-financial indicators to give a more balanced and forecasting power to the traditional financial performance assessment system. They present a CSR performance measurement framework based on the adoption of the Balanced Scorecard approach. Taking into account the social indicators suggested by the traditional balanced scorecard views, an extension of its structure is proposed in order to better embody the environmental and social aspects of company performance.

Application of the BSC in Tracking and Measurement of CSR

It should be noted that while modern application of the BSC in finding management solutions is dates from the works of Art Schneiderman (1987), the usage of the knowledge behind the scorecard can be traced back in early 1950s at General Electric. The Canada's Management Accounting (CMA) Guideline Applying the Balanced Scorecard states:

> "Managers can use the Balanced Scorecard as a means to articulate strategy, communicate its details, motivate people to execute plans, and enable executives to monitor results. Perhaps the prime advantage is that a broad array of indicators can improve the decision making that contributes to strategic success. Non-financial measures enable managers to consider more factors critical to long-term performance."

Table 13 presents how to use the BSC in CSR Measurement.

Table 13   How to Use the BSC in CSR Measurement

Just a reminder, this book, "Principles of CSR," bases mainly on the stakeholders' theory and approach to CSR as the backbone of all what is discussed. Therefore the BSC is demonstrated from a stakeholder perspective.

Using the BSC to measure corporate social responsibility was brought into the limelight by Dow's Sustainability Index in early 1990s. By 2003, this strategic management tool was officially declared to supplement the measurement of CSR based on the Triple Bottom Line measurement. To design a BSC, it is important to first identify a small number of financial and non-financial measures and attach targets to each of them. In this way, when they are reviewed it is possible to determine whether the current performance "meets expectations." This will help to alert managers about areas where performance deviates from expectations and consequently encourage them to focus their attention on these areas to improve the performance within that part.

The details about how to use the BSC are beyond the scope of this book. However, they are well illustrated by books and articles referring to balanced scorecards and design process elements. As much as the BSC helps focus to managers' attention on strategic issues and the management of the implementation of CSR strategy, it is important to remember that the balanced scorecard itself has no role in the formation of a CSR strategy, though it can comfortably co-exist with strategic planning systems and other tools (like the BCG Matrix, McKinsey 7S' Analysis, SWOT, etc.).

4.4 COMMUNICATING CORPORATE SOCIAL RESPONSIBILITY UNDERTAKINGS TO STAKEHOLDERS

After implementing (undertaking) corporate social responsibility activities, it is necessary to track and measure their progress using the tools identified in 4.3, above, or by way of any other recommended tool (depending on industry guidelines and specifics). Thereafter, you have to communicate with the stakeholders (either internal or external). CSR Communication can be taken to mean a set of initiatives that are employed by a company so as to inform, activate, share, as well as dialogue with its concerned stakeholders about what such a company or firm has done or plans to do (or a combination of these) in a given period as regards to CSR. However, it's important to note that CSR communications are voluntary. They can take the form of company reports, press releases, magazines, etc. (Katamba and Gisch-Boie, 2008). CSR communications may be released through a variety of communication channels. These can include (though not limited to) websites, TV, print, radio, or points of sale (CSR Europe (2000a, b). As noted by Birth and others (2008), websites, advertising and social reports play a crucial role compared to others medium/channels.

Figure 2 presents corporate social responsibility communication channels and forms in Uganda.

CSR Communication channels used by studied companies (%)

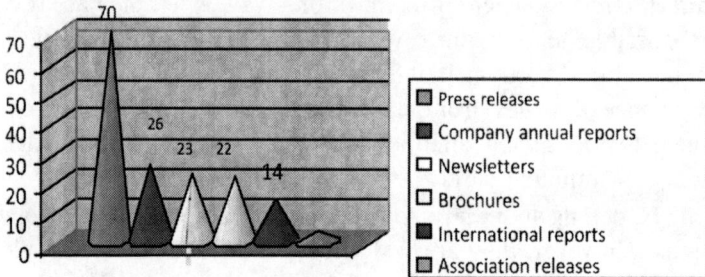

Figure 2—CSR Communication Channels and Forms in Uganda

In Uganda, research by Katamba and Gisch-Boie (2008) reveals that 70% of companies prefer to use press releases as a channel to communicate their CSR activities, because they believe it is the most effective channel. Annual reports take the second most popular position (26%), followed by newsletters (23%), brochures (22%) and international company reports (14%). It's quite surprising that they make less use (4%) of their associations' publications to communicate CSR activities. That is, association releases account for only 4% of all CSR communications.

Regardless of the medium/channel used to communicate a company's CSR undertakings to stakeholders, it is essential to observe transparency and accountability standards for the resources allocated, along with other basic rules of communication (see Table 14 and Table 15). This is because not all the stakeholders are fully aware of what the company undertook in CSR in a particular timeframe (for

Table 14   CSR Communications at The CRH

We maintain our open-door policy with key stakeholder groups. At Group level, we discuss our CSR performance with the investor community, third-party rating agencies and other interested parties. At company level we are in regular dialogue with our employees, local communities, authorities and permitting agencies, underlining our commitment to operate as a good neighbor. Our previous CSR Report was downloaded some 15,000 times from our website and we met requests for close to 10,000 hard copies, printed in eleven languages. We hope that this report will be even more widely disseminated among all our stakeholders.

Source: Sustainable Performance and Growth—The CRH Corporate Social Responsibility Report 2007, p. 3.

Table 15   The Core Research Article for CSR Communications

Birth Gregory, Illia Laura, Lurati Francesco and Zamparini Alessandra (2008), Communicating CSR: practices among Switzerland's top 300 companies, Corporate Communications: An International Journal Vol. 13, No. 2, 2008, pp. 182–196

About the article:
It describes the elements that should be considered in order to develop an effective CSR communication. It also highlights the elements and synergies between issues, objectives, and channels; criteria for a credible social report; the exploitation of the potentialities of CSR advertising and the web; and the understanding of the national context where the organization is operating.

example, by the end of a financial year). A tendency of communicating CSR undertakings simply to win public favor or present half-information is not ethical. This can even have far reaching effects on the communicating company, including litigation, loss of fame and reputation, and/or reductions in customer loyalty. Given this fact, it's important to different CSR Communications from Public Relations and marketing campaigns. This can be briefly shown in Table 16 (on the following page).

Using a "CSR Report" As a CSR Communication Medium

Amongst the CSR communication media, there lays a "CSR Report." This report provides a written detailed documentation of what CSR initiatives and activities have transpired in a given period, such as at the end of a financial or calendar year. This report

Table 16   Differentiations between CSR Communications, Public Relations and Marketing Communications

CSR Communications	Public Relations	Marketing Campaign Communication
A set of initiatives that are employed by a company so as to inform, activate, share as well as dialogue with its concerned stakeholders about what such a company or firm has done, plans to do or a combination of these, in a given period, as regards to CSR.	Building awareness and a favorable image for a company, its products or clients so as to have goodwill. In other words, its one of the promotional tools a company can use.	A specific, defined series of activities used in marketing a new or changed product or service, or in using new marketing channels and method. http://www.entrepreneur.com

can be produced by a company (e.g., XZY, Ltd's CSR Report), an industry (e.g., a Mining industry CSR Report), or a group of stakeholders. It is important to note that different names may be used to refer to a CSR Report. These include: Corporate Responsibility Report; Corporate Citizenship Report; Sustainability Report; etc. It is vital to note that each of these terms, when used as a report heading, means something to the stakeholders. The reader may refer to Chapter One of this book to examine the differences in order to limit expectations from such a report.

Regardless of which term is used, if a corporate social responsibility report is issued, it should be released through a recognized CSR communication medium; various oversight bodies provide industry, sector, or particular business guidelines/criteria to follow so as to make the CSR Report meet the readers' (or targeted audience's) expectations. Examples of such bodies and/or standards include the Global Reporting Initiatives (GRI) Guidelines, OECD Guidelines (for multi-nationals), The UN Global Compact 10 Principles (for companies that signed up with UN Global Compact), Dow Jones Sustainability Index (for companies that are listed on stock exchange), etc. A very challenging scenario may arise when a company has not signed up with any CSR related body, is not listed on any stock exchange, and is not a multi-national organization, etc. Should such a company write and release a CSR Report, selection of necessary content and the proper release medium may be more difficult. In this case, or otherwise, Musikanski (2009) made a proposal of the criteria to guide in communicating CSR undertakings through a CSR Report. The criteria she suggests (as seen from Table 17 below) gives an indication of the basic structure such communication should observe. Specifically, it must be: Audited; Consistent and Comparable; Importance (hierarchical); Inclusive; Relevant, Reliable, Timely, and Clear. Stakeholder interaction is facilitated when the report also addresses Sustainability and Transparency. It is therefore important that any CSR report observes the following criteria as adopted from Musikanski (2009), though more especially when using a corporate report (e.g., an annual report). Table 17 presents the proposed criteria to observe when writing corporate social responsibility report.

Musikanski's proposal was developed after an in-depth review of different authoritative bodies relating to CSR. These included: OECD, UN Global Compact, Generally Accepted Accounting Principles (GAAP), KPMG, PricewaterhouseCoopers, World Bank, IMF, and many more. We therefore find the criteria given as very useful and hence worth adopting when communicating corporate social responsibility undertakings.

4.5 CONCLUSION

This chapter has presented a detailed view of how to implement corporate social responsibility, how to measure as well as monitor progress, and the different tools and indices available for these purposes. It has concluded with how such progress can be communicated to stakeholders so as to keep them informed, and secure their continued involvement or engagement. Due to increasing pressure globally on companies to present their CSR reports, much attention has been put on the "CSR report" to prepare companies how to better absorb this pressure.

4.6 LEARNING ASSIGNMENTS

1. After visiting the website "http://www.mhcinternational.com/," or reading through the book (or an article extract) by Michael Hopkins (MHCi): A Planetary Bargain: Corporate Social Responsibility Comes of Age (Macmillan, UK, 1998), do you think CRITICS provides an ideal measure of CSR?
2. When compared with the Balanced Score Card, which of the two CSR assessments/measuring tools is most ideal?

Table 17   Table Showing Proposed Criteria to Observe When Writing a CSR Report

Criteria	Analysis
Audited so as to ensure monitoring and verification.	In 2005, KPMG' (an international auditing firm) revealed that majority of CSR reports that are audited by a third party, are audited by one of the financial auditing firms. However, third party auditing of CSR reports is not yet the norm. The consensus is that neutral third party auditing will ensure businesses to comply with certain CSR standards. Factors to consider when deciding how to monitor and verify are the focus or likelihood of focus, the public will have on operations. If there are a lot of non-governmental organizations around an issue, such as labor standards, it might be better to use a third party to audit. The AA1000 and SA8000 frameworks are based on monitoring and verifying.
Consistent and Comparable: information that can be compared across time and with other businesses	The GRI sets out a format for each aspect of CSR performance and provides indicators for them. One of the criticisms of CSR frameworks is that there are not enough quantitative indicators. As the field progresses, it is hoped better indicators will emerge. A business manager is better off formulating quantitative indicators when there is no measurement or only qualitative ones exist. This way the manager will better communicate with employees, shareholders and the board of directors.
Importance: Potential impact on stakeholders.	A large business will have a large number of stakeholders and hence it should prove its responsibility and importance to them.
Inclusive: Covers topics important to stakeholders	In industries where risk is a big factor, addressing environmental and social concerns can build confidence with customers, governmental agencies and other stakeholders. Ariva is an example of a business using environmental and social reporting to strengthen its position in the market place and to re-enforce the stewardship working at the company means for employees. Ben and Jerry's is one of the most inclusive reports, but the report risks not being understood by some stakeholders. McDonald's Switzerland offers a solution by issuing three levels of reports: a poster, booklet and in depth report.

Table 17 Table Showing Proposed Criteria to Observe When Writing a CSR Report (Continued)

Relevant, Reliable, Timely, and Clear: present information of value to the reader in a way the reader understand	Starbucks does a good job of balancing the concerns of Wall street, scientists and green roots advocacy group.
Stakeholder interaction: supports relationships between the stakeholders and management	Stakeholder interactions can be used as part of verification and monitoring process, to partner for solutions to business and world problems and to stave adversarial attacks.
Sustainability: incremental improvements towards sustainability.	Integration into the finance, operations, marketing and strategic management of a company is one way to demonstrate incremental improvements towards sustainability. Goal setting is another. Goals set in a CSR report and reported on in subsequent years allow a stakeholder to see a company progress towards sustainability.
Transparent about businesses practices and programs for implementing CSR activities	Collaboration with stakeholders is one way to practice transparency with some constituents. Another way is to report violations of labor standards or environmental laws. Coca-cola Enterprises practices the latter, Gap reported labor violations in its report.

Source: Reproduced with permission from, Laura Musikanski (2009), *Tools for issuing a successful CSR report*, http://www.zipcon.net/~laura/csr_reportsn.htm, accessed, Tuesday, December 15, 2009.

Please suggest reasons for your arguments. It's advisable that you access the articles: Aravossis, K., Panayiotou, N., and Tsousi, K. (2006); and, Panayiotou Nikolaos A., Aravossis Konstantin G., and Moschou Peggy (2009), so that you make a more informed argument.

4.7 REFERENCES

Aravossis, K., Panayiotou, N., Tsousi, K. (2006). A proposed methodological framework for the evaluation of corporate social responsibility. In K. Aravossis, C. A. Brebbia, E. Kakaras, E. and Kungolos, A.G. (Eds.), *Environmental Economics and Investment Assessment*, (pp. 87–95). Shouthampton, Boston: WIT Press.

CSR Europe. (2000a). *The First Ever European Survey of Consumers' Attitude on Corporate Social Responsibility,* CSR Europe Publications, Brussels.

CSR Europe. (2000b). *Communicating Corporate Social Responsibility,* CSR Europe Publications, Brussels.

GTZ BACKUP Initiative Toolkit (2007). BACKUP ("Building Alliances—Creating Knowledge—Updating Partners")—a toolkit created by Deutsche Gesellschaft für Technische Zusammenarbeit (GTZ) and the World Health Organization (WHO) to guide optimum responses to HIV, tuberculosis, malaria and other priority diseases in resource-limited settings. Monitoring and Evaluation definition: Chapter 9, p. 3.

Kaplan, R. S. and Norton, D. P. (1996). "Using the balanced scorecard as a strategic management system," *Harvard Business Review,* Jan–Feb, pp. 75–85.

Kaplan, R. S. and Norton, D. P. (2000). *The Strategy Focused Organization,* HBS Press, USA.

Katamba, D. and Gisch-Boie, S. (2008). *CSR in Uganda: Perceptions, approaches and needs of companies.* http://www.livingearth.org.uk/africa_programmes/uganda/CSR_study.pdf, accessed 20th January, 2009.

Musikanski, L. (2009). *Tools for Issuing a Successful CSR Report.* http://www.zipcon.net/~laura/csr_reportsn.htm, accessed, Tuesday, December 15, 2009.

Panayiotou, N. A., Aravossis, K. G., Moschou, P. (2009). *A New Methodology Approach for Measuring Corporate Social Responsibility Performance, Water, Air, & Soil Pollution:* Focus, Volume 9, Numbers 1–2/April.

4.8 BIBLIOGRAPHY

Allen, J. (2008), *AMICE CSR Conference,* Paris 23–24, October 2008.

Mattsson, B. and Olsson, P. 2001. "Environmental audits and life cycle assessment," in Dillon, M. and Griffith, C. (Eds). *Auditing in the Food Industry—From Safety and Quality to Environmental and Other Audits.* Woodhead Publishing.

Harrison, L. (1995). *Environmental, Health and Safety Auditing Handbook,* Second Edition, McGraw Hill, New York (1995)

ISO 14011, *Audit Procedures and Auditing of Environmental Management Systems.*

Kaplan, R. S. and Norton, D. P. (1996). *The Balanced Scorecard: Translating Strategy into Action,* Harvard Business School Press.

Nelson, D. D. (1998). *International Environmental Auditing,* Government Institutes Inc., USA.

Unhee, K. (1997). *Environmental & Safety Auditing: Program Strategies for Legal, International, and Financial Issues,* CRC Press, Florida.

5

Globalization and Corporate Social Responsibility

Annet K. Nabatanzi Muyimba.

5.1 INTRODUCTION

As world economies continue to integrate, corporate social responsibility and behavior concerns gain momentum. Globalization comes with not only positive effects but also with negative ones. One of the key negative effects is the increase in social irresponsibility of multinational corporations in their bid to maximize profits against society's well being. While social irresponsibility and unethical behavior of companies operating in domestic markets can be controlled by national governments, the global political and legal environment is different and complex. Globalization has reduced the power of national governments to effectively regulate activities of companies that operate beyond and across borders. Secondly, global businesses face a regulatory gap or extra political and legal regulation in different markets or countries. Thirdly, there is yet no universal legal framework to control activities of global businesses. Ultimately, various scholars and policy makers have picked strategic interest in ethical and social responsibility in order to discover alternative solutions to close the gaps, which can be traced back as far as 1970s. Therefore, the chapter will concentrate on understanding the relationship between globalization and corporate social responsibility, consequences and the possible strategic solution.

LEARNING OBJECTIVES

The main aim of this chapter is to introduce the concept of Corporate Social Responsibility at the global business scale with a focus on

69

strategies of Global corporate social responsibility management, the key CSR issues and drivers in global business operations. The barriers to effective Global corporate social responsibility implementation at the global level are also addressed. At the end of this chapter, students will be able to assess global CSR situations and select the appropriate CSR approaches and strategies to use.

SUBTOPICS COVERED:

1. Introduction to "Globalization"
2. Global Corporate Social Responsibility (GCSR)
3. Approaches to Global CSR
4. Drivers of Global CSR
5. Benefits and Implications of Global CSR Management
6. Factors that Hinder Implementation of CSR in Global Markets
7. Strategies for Global CSR Management
8. Global CSR Cases

5.2 INTRODUCTION TO "GLOBALIZATION"

5.2.1 Basic Knowledge about Globalization

There is no single all-encompassing definition of "globalization" and it has become a broad topic or term to mean a multitude of global interactions. Examples of such meanings and definitions include the widening and deepening of international flows of trade, finance, and information into a single, integrated global market. Globalization has also been defined as a process of transformation of local or regional phenomena into global ones. This ideally refers to the process of blending, unifying or homogenizing the people and businesses in the world into a single society and function together. This process takes into consideration the economic, technological, socio-cultural and political forces in the international environment. Globalization comes with the elimination of state involvement in exchanges (goods and services, information, finances, social and human resources) across borders and increasingly integrates the global system of production and exchanges.

The growth of globalization followed the phenomenon of the internationalization of firms after the 1970s, and it is crucial to distinguish the two terms since many times they are confused and used interchangeably. Internationalization is the geographical expansion of business activities over a national or country's border or the increased international involvement of a business, where as globalization is a stage in which the firm's overall operations are managed on a global scale and not just independently operated in a few select countries. Global companies include transnational and/or multinational corporations and companies operating global supply chains. Hence globalization is characterized by worldwide integration of competitive markets and companies facing global competition. Therefore, any company operating in markets world wide (such as global supply chains) and/or facing global competition is a global company.

5.2.2 Drivers of Globalization of Businesses Include

i. The growth of low-cost technologies connecting people and locations. Today there is better information and communication technology (telecommunications, mass media, computers and internet, transportation, etc.) creating greater awareness and accessibility of international business opportunities. For instance companies that have websites and/or internet connectivity are in a better position to access markets beyond their national borders.

ii. Deregulation, privatization, the removal of trade barriers among countries and regions, and the emergence of free trade agreements have resulted into a more level playing field for all firms worldwide. For example, the Africa Growth Opportunity Act (AGOA) allows African firms to export to United States of America. In Uganda, Tri-Star Apparel Company produces finished textile products for the US market.

iii. The widespread economic restructuring and liberalization by many economies after World War II. In addition, the collapse of socialism—mainly in Russia, central and Eastern Europe—has attracted many companies to such economies.

iv. Opening up of markets originally closed through the WTO, as well as geographical expansion of markets in Asia (particularly China) have opened further opportunities for growth and investment. For instance, many American companies such as Nike have relocated their production facilities to China, mainly to take advantage of low cost labor and re-export the finished products to the US market.

v. The growth of interdependent and global risks such as global warming, terrorism, weapons of mass destruction and diseases, etc., whose effects do not stop at national borders but affect the lives of many people across the globe. Hence, their resolution calls for collective efforts from different communities throughout the world.

On one side, globalization is credited for its positive effects to economies worldwide in various ways, ranging from industrial, financial, economic, political, competition, and technological, cultural, technical and legal and/or ethical benefits. However, on the other side, globalization comes also with problems such as environmental degradation, disease, "brain-drain," food and water insecurity, drugs, child and animal trafficking and others.

In particular, this chapter will concentrate on understanding corporate irresponsibility as a consequence of globalization. Contrary to earlier principles of CSR, which were based on the assumption that responsible firms operate within properly defined political and legal frameworks by a single government, with the growth in globalization that assumption does not hold any more. The global political and legal framework is different and more complex. Today, businesses operating in a global environment will often face regulatory gaps, extra political and legal rules and regulations, and/or new social and environmental challenges. In addition, globalization of businesses reduces the power of national governments to regulate the activities of companies that operate beyond and across borders.

5.3 Global Corporate Social Responsibility (GCSR)

5.3.1 Brief Revisit of Corporate Social Responsibility in a Global Perspective

The concept of corporate social responsibility stems from a business philosophy with a societal concept/orientation. The societal business orientation (otherwise referred to as "stakeholder orientation") works toward balancing the needs of the company with those of customers and society in general in an ethical manner. It is because of today's increasingly globalize marketplace that there is increasing demand for ethical, environmentally friendly and socially responsible business processes and acts.

Historically, the economic interests of businesses surpassed interests in business ethics and societal needs. Traditionally, it has been assumed that the government sets the rules and regulations that direct and control the consequences of business exchanges and ensures contribution to the well being of society. However, as corporations pursue growth through globalization, they encounter new and different challenges that limit their growth and profit potential. The challenges may be social, cultural, economic, political, environmental, legal or technological such as peace, crime, migration, production, employment and income distribution.

Therefore, past assumptions may not hold in the event of globalization due to three main reasons. First, through globalization the national government loses its power and control over businesses that have expanded their activities beyond its borders. Secondly, new social and environmental challenges arise that cannot be controlled by a single government entity—for instance, global warming, crime, terrorism, and disease. Third, the presence of international organizations and frameworks such as NGOs, civil society groups, international laws and courts, whose activities are not limited to a particular territory, will impinge upon global businesses.

Consequently, there has been a drastic acceleration in most company's strategic interest in ethical and social responsibility that can be traced back to the 1980s and 1990s. Today, however, the range and quantity of business ethical and social responsibility issues reflects the degree to which business is perceived to be at odds with non-economic social values within major national corporations and multinationals—hence the birth and popularity of corporate social responsibility. For instance, major corporate websites now routinely carry information about their commitment to promoting non-economic social values such as ethical codes and social responsibility charters. In other cases, companies have re-branded and re-positioned their core values to emphasize social responsibility. A good example is the BP petroleum company tagline "beyond petroleum," indicating an increased environmental concern.

Corporate social responsibility management has both long- and short-term components that can result in a long term company investment in activities aimed at maintaining its relationships within society. On the other hand, CSR can also involve short term activities and plans to handle sudden and/or critical crises or incidents that may be affecting the company. Thus, the act and process of handling crises and incidents affecting a company is referred to as CSR Recovery, while the day-to-day and continuous management of CSR is known as CSR Enforcement. In addition, CSR activities may be planned and implemented in the domestic and/or international or foreign markets of a company. The latter concept is what is known as Global Corporate Social Responsibility (GCSR).

The two main perspectives of any global corporate strategy are: (1) focusing on identifying differences among foreign markets, which gives rise to the adaptation of CSR activities to the conditions of each host country; and (2) focusing on similarities among foreign markets, which gives rise to standardization of CSR activities across markets with limited tactical variations required, depending upon the differences in environmental forces in each host country.

Table 18   Global Corporate Strategy and CSR—Key Challenges

In both perspectives a global corporate strategy, CSR management and strategy focuses on identifying and suggesting solutions to two major challenges.

i. Developing and managing relationships with society through the interplay of actors, activities and resources.

ii. Capability to handle both the unexpected incidents and the long term reduction of gaps between stakeholders' expectations and the company performance.

5.3.2 The Emergence of Global Corporate Social Responsibility (GCSR) and Its Effects

The traditional view of social responsibility is clearly divided between the main actors: civil society, government, and business. These actors contribute solidarity, power and money respectively and through their interactions; society forms shared values, tradition and cultural associations (solidarity). Governments, by formulating and enforcing laws, provide a mechanism for conflict management and resolution. Businesses, through their activities, improve the well being of society by providing goods, jobs, and the payment of taxes. However, with globalization this division of labor seems to erode, making social responsibility a challenge. Globalization has weakened the power of nations (political authorities) to regulate the activities of corporations that globally expand their activities. According to Habermas (2001) this has resulted into two major effects:

i. Race to the bottom effect: With globalization, multinationals in search of cost advantages split and shift their operations to those regions that offer profit maximization. They deliberately determine the places that minimize tax burdens, as well as those that minimize the direct costs of producing goods. Since multinationals can choose between regions and/or countries in which to produce and pay taxes, governments are forced into a race to the bottom in order to attract and win competitive corporate investments against other countries. This reduces the incentive of public authorities to set rules, regulate economic activities, and enforce specific behaviors within their jurisdictions.

ii. Regulatory vacuum effect: Due to globalization the world is confronted with transnational challenges such as global warming, corruption, HIV/AIDS, human rights and ecological problems in general. These are, in one way or another, caused by multinational expansion. However, these problems cannot be solved by a single government or authority within a national state, and there is as of yet no sufficient global governance institution that defines and imposes rules and regulations for coping with these challenges. Hence, these effects create challenges in enforcement of global corporate social responsibility.

GCSR addresses both the responsible and irresponsible acts necessitating both enforcement and recovery strategies with equal importance. CSR, as a relationship between the company and society, includes: ethical behaviors; business effects on the natural environment; adherence to international laws and regulations; disclosure of investments, codes and standards; and the interferences of businesses with established social and human rights. CSR on global scale addresses challenges at the macro level, which refers to the indirect consequences of economic activities of Multinationals or global companies for the host country and society beyond their home base countries. Finally, micro CSR encompass the immediate effects on local communities of the global company in each individual country.

Social responsibility at global scale in the first place requires that a company accounts for its actions hence Social accounting, auditing and reporting which results into a social performance standard. Social accounting/reporting/disclosure is a concept that refers to the communication of social and environmental effects of the company's economic actions to the host country, particular interest groups within society and to society at large. Social reporting is an important corporate social responsibility element and is becoming an international legal and ethical requirement for all companies. Social accounting and reporting also emphasizes transparency of investments.

For that matter a number of guidelines, standards, and international bodies have been created to provide frameworks for social accounting, auditing, reporting and monitoring. (For details, refer to Chapters Four and Six.) However, a quick summary shows examples such as: Global Reporting Initiative's Sustainability Reporting Guidelines; Good Corporation; Green Global Certification; the ISO 14000 Environmental Management Standard; Social Accountability International SA8000; the International Criminal Court; the United Nations Global Compact (which requires companies to report in the format of the Compact's ten universal principles); and the United Nations' Eco-Efficiency indicators for International Standards of Accounting and Reporting, etc.

In addition to the above list, many nations have put in place their own legal requirements for social accounting, auditing and reporting—for instance, the French "Bilan Social" (Social Balance Sheet). In Uganda such legal requirements are embedded in Acts such as Public Procurement and Disposal Act, the Company Act, the Financial and Accountability Act, etc. However, the challenge with social reporting is the difficult in securing agreement on meaningful measurements of the social and environmental performance of companies across nations. Although several companies today do produce externally audited annual reports that cover Sustainable Development and CSR, the reports have been widely criticized and dismissed for lack of objectivity. Cases of such include Enron's annual CSR report and the Tobacco corporations' social reports. On the positive side, much success has been achieved globally in having companies include warning labels for products that are potentially dangerous in all communications to their customers and public in general. For instance, all tobacco and alcohol manufacturers are now bound by such disclosure laws.

5.3.3 Features of a Global Corporate Social Responsibility (GCSR) Firm

According to Ackerman (1975) there are three features that characterize a socially responsible firm globally that is: 1) the capacity to monitor and assess environmental conditions; 2) the capacity to attend to the many demands of numerous stakeholders and 3) competence in designing and implementing plans and policies to respond to changing conditions. However, Forstater and others (2010) characterize global CSR in terms of goals. In that regard, Global CSR constitutes the response to social and environmental issues; setting professional and proactive approaches to their business impacts, measurement and reporting of performance; and targeting their strategies towards sustainable development with in society. Others have related it to the level of CSR decision making whether headquarter or individual subsidiaries; nature of CSR issues whether Micro or Macro, and others in terms of standardized or localization of activities. Therefore, it is possible to find different classifications of what characterizes Global CSR, but what seems to matters more are the goals and mechanisms for implementation.

Although, the principles of corporate social responsibility may be applicable to all sizes and types of companies with minor differences due to cultural complexities, there is still a general lack of universally accepted measures of social performance. In addition, the level of social performance of global companies may differ from country to country or from one region to another. At a global scale, companies considered to be socially responsible are those that proactively identify, prevent and solve problems they cause, compile to both national and international laws, think and behave ethically, and meet both economic and social expectations of their stakeholders (Ofori and Hinson, 2007; Jones, Comfort and Hillier, 2007). However, due to growing global competition, compliance to laws is no longer effective in impressing consumers and other stakeholders. Certainly, global companies need to increase their commitment to and engagement with society and other stakeholders.

In recent developments, the Global Responsible Competitiveness Index in 2007, revealed that more advanced economies do better than developing countries in terms of responsible business practices. Sweden tops the list, followed by Denmark. The list for the top 20 countries is dominated by Europe and North America, Australia, New Zealand, Japan and Hong Kong, with no African country yet among the top. Despite the fact that China and India recorded high levels of pollution and reluctant human rights, environment and labor standards, China has designed sustainable energy, cities and industrial systems to promote socially responsible practices. In 2008, China launched the CSR guidelines for state-owned companies with emphasis on payment of taxes, ethics, workers rights, environmental protection and social development. Despite these efforts, Chinese enterprises operating in overseas markets especially in Africa have been accused of natural resource exploitation without providing sustainable remedies. On the other hand advanced countries have been criticized for relocating their more dirty and hazardous industries to other parts of the world where there are less stringent environmental and social standards. For example, up to 40 percent of air pollution in the Pearl River Delta in China is attributed to manufacturing exports to Europe and North America.

In Kenya, river Ngiro has experienced reduced water levels due to large scale water supply to companies producing flowers for exports. In another related account, a World Bank economist, Lawrence Summers commented that advanced countries dump toxic waste and expired and low quality products in African countries. He further argues that under-populated countries in Africa, which should be vastly under-polluted, however, have disproportionately low quality air compared to highly populated cities in advanced countries. This indicates the gravity of the CSR problems in Africa, and the increasing vulnerability of developing countries in general to corporate social irresponsibility. On firm size analysis, big and multinational companies are at an advantage in implementing CSR activities compared to small one. This has been attributed to resource advantage and global experience enjoyed by the larger companies.

5.4 APPROACHES TO GLOBAL CORPORATE SOCIAL RESPONSIBILITY

There are two major approaches to corporate social responsibility by corporations operating in a global environment. First and foremost is the community-based development approach, where companies get actively involved in community developments. For example, Shell Foundations is involved in the Flower Valley, South Africa, where they have set up an Early Learning Center to educate the community's children, in addition to developing new skills for the adults. The MTN Foundation joined with Habitat for Humanity to build houses in a number of under privileged communities in Africa. Many other global corporations are involved in the establishment of education and health facilities, especially HIV/AIDS projects. In Africa, these include such entities as Microsoft Melinda and Bill Gates Foundation, the Aga Khan Foundation, etc.

The other common approach to corporate social responsibility by global companies is through extending aid to local organizations and impoverished communities in developing countries. The disadvantage to this approach is that it negates skills development, whereas community-based development promotes more sustainable development through skills improvement and development. According to a survey by Fleishman-Hillard (2006), in the United States of America, companies' charitable and philanthropic giving is no longer good enough strategy to consumers' loyalty. It is considered "a bare standard expectation or a bare minimum" for consumers in rating socially responsibility. However, employee benefits and community volunteering topped the list of standards by which consumers judge excellence in corporate responsibility. In Africa, in particular, the most common approach to CSR is Philanthropic support mainly towards education, health (HIV/AIDS projects), environment, sports and cultural events and skills development. On the other hand, Chinese companies operating in Africa tend to emphasize local community and infrastructural development while Western Multinationals put more emphasis on revenue transparency compliance and capacity development of public institutions.

5.5 DRIVERS OF GLOBAL CORPORATE SOCIAL RESPONSIBILITY

Transnational or multinational Corporations adopt corporate social responsibility practices due to several factors, including the following:

i. Market or environmental forces

Companies operating in many countries and different markets encounter new and different challenges in each that impose limitations on their market growth and profits. Such forces include government regulations and policies, taxes, natural environmental restrictions and standards, social and cultural differences, as well as varying labor laws and ethical requirements. As a result companies must proactively comply with and respond to such standards and requirements. Sometimes it is the global competition itself that forces companies to examine their importance and contribution to community and national development. Companies may also use CSR as a strategic and competitive tool to gain quick public support for their presence and to sustain their competitive positions globally through their social contributions. For instance in 2009, 35 percent of Saudi Arabian companies had plans or had already launched innovative offerings with enhanced social and environmental performance.

ii. Increased involvement and investment in developing countries

In the current Global Environment many multinational corporations (MNCs) have relocated their production facilities to less developed countries in order to maximize profits as a result of location advantages. These include cheap labor and raw materials, weak unions, and low taxes. MNCs have enormous resources, which makes them economical and socially influential in the development of many underdeveloped countries. Some of these companies have resources which are bigger or equal to the total gross domestic product of some of their host countries (Chandler and Mazlish, 2005). Consequently, many of these countries' governments have deliberately established programs to attract and compete for corporate investments. In addition, MNCs have increased their sourcing of products and services from developing countries, and as a result these companies have found it increasingly their responsibility to contribute to the economic and social development of these regions.

For example, many developing countries in Africa, Latin America and Asia encounter both social and economic problems. The economic setbacks include low incomes, unemployment, high inflation, weak currencies and capital flight, which factors explain high levels of poverty in many developing countries. Hence, the presence of extreme poverty in these nations places a special social responsibility on global businesses to contribute to sustainable economic and social development that would help alleviate the poverty.

iii. Laws and regulations

Corporate social responsibility is driven globally by governments and other independent pressure groups. It's the role of governments to ensure that companies do not harm people, their social arrangements, and the environment. Therefore, governments set the CSR agenda through policies, laws and regulations which require businesses to operate and behave responsibly. For instance, it is a legal requirement for all companies to pay taxes to the government, which taxes are in turn used to provide social services and to monitor the business activities to ensure that society and the environment are not adversely affected. A good example of a country that has enacted laws on CSR is Denmark, which adopted a law on December 16, 2008, making it mandatory for the largest companies, investors, and state owned companies to include information on CSR in their annual financial reports. However, for most countries CSR is still voluntary, even in Denmark where it is a legal requirement that companies with no policy on CSR state it explicitly in their annual financial reports. Some of the CSR information required in the annual reports includes: the company's CSR policies, socially responsible investments (SRI); practically implemented policies; CSR/SRI results obtained and future expectations or projections.

iv. Critical crises and consequences

In some cases, companies are forced to adopt a CSR program as a result of a crisis—especially unethical behavior and/or environmental mismanagement. One of the most prominent examples of this in recent times was the Chinese Baby powdered milk contaminated with melamine. This led to the death of many babies, a ban on importation of the milk by many countries, and eventually the prosecution, conviction, and death sentences of the managers involved. Other global examples include the lead poisoning prone paint used by the giant toy company Mattel, which led to a recall of millions of toys globally and Toyota's 2010 recall of thousands of cars with malfunctioning engines. These and other similar incidents have motivated many companies to initiate new risk management and quality control processes.

v. The battle for talent

The growing consideration of employee interests as the first priority for many organizations is not only a result of strict labor laws, but also a result of the business benefits that can be enjoyed from improved and fair employee treatment. Such benefits include employee loyalty, quality recruitment, retention, and higher productivity. Global companies strategically invest in workforce-related social responsibility areas, in part, to win employees with the best talents. According to Saudi Arabia's Responsible Competitiveness Report of 2009, for a company to win talent it must be admired, and to be admired the company must be a responsible employer. This is normally achieved through offering the best employee benefits and creating opportunities for women and other vulnerable groups in the work force, and by rewarding employees in ways that allow them to show their talents.

vi. Stakeholder interests

Companies today are motivated to become more socially responsible due to pressure from their stakeholders and as a result of global human rights awareness and movements. External stakeholders include customers, consumers, investors, regulators, and the media. Non-governmental organizations, through their education and dialogue programs, have increased social awareness of communities. This has resulted in more pressure and demand for companies to behave more responsibly. The media is also playing a big role in scrutinizing businesses' actions, ethical and CSR policies.

vii. Growth in companies ethical orientations

Maintaining ethical behavior in business transactions is a requirement by many governments today. There is a notion that humans are built with the capacity to cheat and manipulate others. Therefore, since businesses are operated by human beings there is always a need to reduce dirty dealings, which attract fines and damage companies' reputations. In a bid to avoid breaking government laws, companies have proactively integrated CSR in their strategic plans and voluntarily changed their behavior and culture. This in turn has resulted in increased internal ethics training of employees to be able to make ethical decisions, including setting and integrating CSR goals and values in their strategic plans.

viii. Global environmental risks

Recent years have witnessed increasing concerns for the preservation of the global natural environment. This is especially linked to the increased depletion of limited natural resources, degradation of the environment, and the most recent concerns about global warming and diseases due to industrialization. The increase in World population, and hence consumer demand, has exerted more pressure on nature and non-renewable resources. However, as a result of communication technology and globalization, consumers worldwide are becoming more aware of the environmental and social implications of their purchase decisions. Hence, the growing demands for environmentally friendly products. Consequently, many consumer groups promote the purchase of products that are socially, ethically and environmentally friendly. This, on the other hand, has forced multinational companies to engage and invest in CSR activities to control and reduce on the effects of their products and activities on society and the environment.

5.6 BENEFITS AND IMPLICATIONS OF GLOBAL CSR MANAGEMENT

The nature and number of benefits of CSR for any company varies according to the nature of the enterprise, and these often go beyond financial benefits. Therefore we can examine the benefits and implications of Global CSR management, including:

i. Business Growth and Profitability: Corporate social responsibility has been enforced for corporate benefits such as business growth and profitability, especially when the business makes long-term investments to maintain its relationship with society.

ii. Corporate Reputation and Market Position: When a company connects to society through maintaining and enforcing CSR activities, the result is a positive public image. If a critical incident (such as corruption or environmental scandal) is not handled well from the stakeholders' point of view, it may negatively affect the firm's reputation. However, if the incident is skillfully handled, the negative effects could be minimized and possibly recovered in a short time. Therefore, proactive CRS plans and programs can be used to manage such risks or incidents that may arise, and which normally draw the attention of regulators, courts, governments and media. CSR contributes positively to the perception of the company among the general public, especially when the staff get involved in the community through giving, fundraising activities and community volunteering.

iii. Human Resource Management: CSR is a key factor that may greatly influence human resource recruitment and retention within the competitive employee market. CSR policy is an often asked question during interviews, and having an attractive CSR policy (especially one that benefits employees) is a substantial advantage in recruiting and retaining the best employees. It also results into increased staff commitment, productivity and involvement.

iv. Brand Value: CSR is reported to be beneficial in very competitive markets as a tool to create, develop and sustain global brand differentiation and trust. This is accomplished through winning public support, customer loyalty based on the company's ethical values, integrity and best practices, and contributions to social development.

v. Good Relationships with Governments and Communities: Enhanced relationships follow when many companies voluntarily engage in CSR activities to avoid government interference. Their voluntary CSR involvement can persuade the government and the public to think that these companies take issues such as health and safety, labor and environment seriously and will act as good corporate citizens.

vi. Development of closer links with customers and greater awareness of their needs. Consumers can and will readily reward or punish a company as a result of its CSR status in the community.

5.7 Factors That Hinder Implementation of CSR in Global Markets

Profit Objective of the Firm: First and foremost, it is argued that the main objective of business is to generate profit and maximize returns to shareholders. Scholars such as Friedman (1970) assert that managers are responsible to their shareholders and not to society as a whole, that CSR is incongruent with the purpose of business and a hindrance to free trade. In addition, those corporations should only obey the laws of the countries and pay taxes, which governments should utilize to provide social services. This view hinders implementation of CSR on the argument that businesses are not accountable to society but only to their shareholders. Table 19 presents why corporations are socially responsible in the global society.

i. Company Financial and Political Power:

In the real world, many large companies are involved in exploitive practices, knowingly or unknowingly, through sub-contractors. Therefore, through their finance muscle and increased influence in the political arena, they influence policies in their favor and often go unchecked. Others lobby governments actively

Table 19   Why Corporations Are Socially Responsible in the Global Society

Proponents of CSR (the modern view) argue that corporations are responsible to society because:

• The type of capitalism practiced in developing countries is a form of economic and cultural imperialism, since these countries have fewer labor protections and laws thus citizens are at higher risk of exploitation by Multinational corporations.

• The economy exists to serve human beings hence all economic entities have an obligation to society

• CSR can significantly improve long term profitability of the company because it reduces risks and inefficiencies and generates other benefits.

to prevent competition, and others have financially aided political parties in host countries.

ii. Differences in Cultural Values:

Differences in cultural values across countries may also hinder the development and implementation of a global CSR agenda. Some communities resist activities undertaken by organizations that seem to change their cultural values, such as keeping a clean, healthy, and hygienic environment.

iii. Lack of Managerial Skills and Commitment:

Management, in many cases, is not properly equipped or trained to handle socially responsible issues and activities. In addition, management is often heavily engrossed with profit-making activities and with contractual commitments to shareholders, who expect maximum returns on investment. Moreover, in some cases CSR may reduce immediate profits.

iv. Inadequate or Lack of Legal and Government Monitoring Systems:

This has contributed to companies going unchecked when involved in unethical or antisocial practices, others have survived payments of compensations and damages to society or governments due to lack of systems to determine the worth of the damages or fines to pay. For instance, in cases of low pay, poor working conditions and human health risks.

v. Lack of a Recognized Standard and Policy for CSR:

Most multinational corporations (MNCs), public sector organizations, and the United Nations, for instance, adhere to the Triple Bottom Line (TBL) principles. It is widely accepted that CSR adheres to similar principles globally. However, there is as of yet no formal act of legislation. In that regard the UN has developed the principles of socially responsible investment (SRI) as guidelines to investing corporations. Furthermore, MNCs were, in the 1970s, criticized for getting involved in various host country's politics. As a consequence, most oil companies currently state that they will remain politically neutral and not intervene in "party politics." Most of these companies also support the universal Declaration of Human rights; they work with non-governmental organizations (NGOs) and international organizations in fighting corruption and bribery

5.8 STRATEGIES FOR GLOBAL CSR MANAGEMENT

In order to deal with both the positive and negative effects of globalization on a company's CSR activities, there are controls or mechanisms to follow:

i. Having in place a governance or company policy on CSR activities and reporting. The implementation of CSR is closely related to the practice of Good Corporate Governance (GCG).

ii. According to Mathew (1997), a redistribution of power between national governments, economic actors, and civil society is necessary. In this new arrangement the role and influence of civil society on large multinational corporations is increased. NGOs become more involved in the decision making processes of governments and corporations. Hence, NGOs direct their activities towards corporations to ensure that transparency prevails among businesses. This has forced corporations to start proactive CSR initiatives such as human rights, health, and other self-regulation initiatives that fill the gap in global governance mentioned above.

iii. The third principle requires that companies pay attention to Stakeholder Theory (Freeman, 1984), which states that as the company does what it has to do for the benefit of the company, it also has to take into consideration the needs of the stakeholders and involve them in decision making process in order to achieve long term company success. According to Vaaland and Heide, (2008) the company should have a system to identify the most significant stakeholders in each incident and their expectations, and be the first to break the story to them.

iv. Adherence to government/national and/or international CSR reporting regulations and standards. This is due to the fact that the extent and nature of corporate social reporting varies between different countries. For instance, in Europe, many countries such as Norway, Sweden, France, Netherlands and Denmark have introduced legislation to increase environmental disclosures by companies. It is also true that companies report more extensively on CSR in advanced economies than in less developed countries in which the same company operates.

v. Having social audit or assurance services performed by an independent external party. This may convince the stakeholders that the report is made in accordance with international reporting standards. However, the auditor needs a CSR auditing standard. The standard is not similar to the auditing standards of financial reports, since CSR reports cover wider aspects and the reports are more qualitative than financial reports (Utama, 2008). However, regulators around the world need to agree on the global CSR reporting standards so that companies in different countries can adhere to the same reporting standards.

vi. According to Birch (2008), global companies need to build corporate citizenship in form of codes of conduct, and/or charters of corporate behavior. These codes and charters are meant to form unified behavioral standards and a corporate culture for every staff employed in the global company. In addition, being a good corporate citizen helps companies to connect and win stakeholders' trust and loyalty compared to their competitors. Birch (2008) further developed a ten point recommendation on how companies can achieve corporate citizenship. These principles focus on developing an understanding of how global companies should engage in corporate activities in the most ethical, supportive and responsible; culturally sensitive and respectful; localized and harmonious manner with the society.

5.9 GLOBAL CSR CASES

i. Shell's 2004 scandal on misreporting of its oil reserves.

According to *The New York Times* in March 2004, shell overestimated its proven oil reserves by 40 percent. The estimates were based on assessments made in May 2000 by the then Director of exploration and developments. As a result, the chairman and the director of exploration were sacked and the Group Chief Financial officer resigned after it was revealed that these executives had knowledge of it but did nothing to correct it. The investigations revealed that approximately 2.3 million barrels of proved reserves were non-complaint. Hence, the failure to disclose, violation of the US securities law and Multiple listing requirements posed reputation and legal challenges to the world's 3rd largest oil company. Shell was charged with hypocrisy and insincerity, which seriously damaged its reputation globally. This scandal substantially damaged the company's reputation, even though Shell had a much publicized CSR policy and was the pioneer in triple bottom line reporting. Since then, Shell foundation has been involved in many projects across the world, including the partnership with Marks and Spencer (UK) in flower and fruit growing communities in South Africa.

ii. The 1989 giant oil spill of Exxon Mobil shipping company.

Exxon Mobil Corporation is the second largest oil and gas company only after BP Petroleum. The company is involved in oil exploration, production, transportation and marketing in more than 200 countries worldwide. Exxon Mobil Corporation was formed out of a merger between Exxon Corporation and Mobil Corporation, which was completed in 1999. The merger was intended to bring about cost savings and maximize profits after the several disasters Exxon Corporation had encountered in the previous decade. In 1989 Exxon experienced one of the biggest vessel crashes of the time. The incident occurred when one of the company's vessels ran aground in Prince William Sound off the Port of Valdez in Alaska. The result was the spilling of 38,800 metric tons of crude oil into the ocean. The timing of the spill, the remoteness of the location (which includes thousands of miles of rugged and wild shoreline, and the rich wildlife), rapidly turned the accident into an environmental disaster. The disaster turned into crisis for the company especially due to the slow response, and failure of the Chief executive officer to visit the site of the crash. Consequently, the disaster was costly amounting to a total of \$4 billion paid out by Exxon in clean-up costs and criminal charges and fines.

iii. Total Oil Company's operations in Burma.

Total started its oil operations in Burma as a virgin market in 1992. Total happens to be the largest public company in France and the Fourth largest oil and gas company in the world. Total oil was the largest foreign investor in Burma by 2000. Total Oil's operations in Burma are conducted on behalf of a military regime blamed for systematic breaches of human rights. There is no independent judiciary in Burma, and political opposition to the military government is not tolerated. The regime is characterized with forced labour and extra judicial killings by troops providing security for the Yadana and Yetagun pipeline in Myanmar. These allegations and violations of human rights forced European Union to passed economic sanctions on Burma. As a result several multinational corporations withdraw their investments from Burma except Total. At times the international community has repeatedly expressed great concern over the situation, and Total's continued involvement in oil exploration and exploitation. However, criticism from the international community and media is constantly counterbalanced by communications from Total Oil. The company claims making a positive contribution to both economic and social development of Burma despite the internal turmoil. The company contribution has been record in terms of employment, public health and micro-credit initiatives, education and infrastructural development. In addition, Total oil has refuted allegations of their involvement in human rights violation contained in the ERI Annual reports. The company has from time to time insisted on implementing its projects in Burma in compliance with local and international legislation and own code of conduct.

5.10 LEARNING ASSIGNMENTS

1. Assess the key global CSR issues in each of the company cases (1–3) above.

2. Select the appropriate CSR management strategies to use in each of the situations above, and show how strategies can be implemented to achieve global competitiveness. (You may find that you have to borrow knowledge from Chapter Five when it comes to implementations issues).

5.11 REFERENCES

Ackerman, R. W. (1975). *The Social Challenge to Business.* Harvard University Press, Cambridge, MA.

Birch, D. (2008). Analysis of CSR: Principles and concepts—Ten principles of corporate citizenship. *Social Responsibility Journal,* Vol. 4, No. 1/2, pp. 129–135.

Blanche, E. (2004). Shell Scandal Points to Exaggerated Estimates of Oil Reserves. Daily Star, 17 April, 2004. www.countercurrents.org/peakoil-blance170404.htm

Carroll, A. B. (1991). *The Pyramid of Corporate Social Responsibility: towards the moral management of organizational stakeholders—balancing economic, legal and social responsibilities.* See: www.findarticles.com/p/articles/ml_m1038/is, No. 4, Vol. 34.

Chevron. (2010). *Corporate Social Responsibility Report.* www.chevron.com/globaissues/corporate responsibility/2010

Crowther, D. and Martinez, E. O. (2007). No Principles and Nothing in Reserves and the Failure of Agency Theory. *Social Responsibility Journal,* Vol. 3, No. 4.

Douglas, A., Doris, J., and Johnson, B. (2004). Corporate Social Reporting in Irish Financial Institutions. *TQM Magazine,* Vol. 16, No. 6. pp. 387–395.

Explore North. (1999). *The Exxon Valdez Oil Spill Disaster. Explore North,* 3/24/1999. www.explorenorth.com/library/weekly/aa032499.htm

Exxon Mobil Company. www.exxonmobil.co.tv

Exxon Valdez Oil Spill: Supreme Court. www.lycos/info/exxon-valdez-oul-spill-supreme-court.html.

Fleishman-Hillard Report (2007). "Rethinking Corporate Social Responsibility" National Consumer League Study, USA.

Freeman, R. (1984). Strategic Management: a stakeholder approach. Pitman.

Freidman, M. (1970). The Social Responsibility of Business Is to Increase Profits. *New York Times Magazine.* See: http://www.colorado.edu/studentgroups/libertarians/issues/friedman-soc-res-business.html.

Global Issues Website. www.globalissues.org/article/723/corporate-social-responsibility.

Jones, P., Hillier, D., and Comfort, D. (2007). Corporate Social Responsibility: a case study of the top ten global retailers. *EuroMed Journal of Business,* Vol. 2, No. 1, pp. 23–35.

Mbathi, I. (2006). *Total in Burma: International University Bremen (Germany)/Starethe Technical Training Institute (Kenya).* Covalence SA, Geneva. www.covalence.ch/docs/total in burma.pdf.

Ofori, D. F. and Hinson, R. E. (2007). Corporate Social Responsibility Perspectives of Leading Firms in Ghana. *Corporate Governance,* Vol. 7, No. 2, pp. 178–193.

Out-Law News. (2004). *E-mail Lifts Lid on Shell Scandal.* www.out-law.com/p.4466

Ruzzier, M., Hisrich, R., and Antonic, B. (2006). SME Internationalization research: past, present and future. *Journal of Small Business and Enterprise Development.* Vol. 13, No. 4, pp. 476–497.

Skjaerseth, J. B., Tangen, K., and Swanson, P. (2004). *Limits to Corporate Social Responsibility: A Comparative Study of Four Major Oil Companies.* Fridtjof Nansen Institute Norway, www.fni.no.

Total Oil. (2009). *Our Response to Allegations Contained in the ERI Report.* www.burma.total.com/publications/Total Response

Total Oil. (2009). *Total in Myanmar Updates,* September, 2009. www.burma.total.com/publications/total in Myanmar-updates

Utama, S. (2008). *Regulations to Enhance Accountable Corporate Responsibility Reporting.* Faculty of Economic University of Indonesia.

Vaaland, T. I. and Heide, M. (2008). Managing Corporate Social Responsibility: lessons from the oil industry. *Corporate communications: an international Journal,* Vol.13, No.2, pp. 212–225.

Visser, W., Matten, D., Pohl, M., and Tolhurst, N. (2007). *The A to Z of Corporate Social Responsibility.* London: Wiley. ISBN 978-0-470-72395-1.

Wartick, S. and Wood, D. J. (1998). *International Business and Society.* Blackwell, Malden, MA.

The State of Responsible Competitiveness 2007: Making Sustainable Development count in global markets. *Accountability.* www.zadek.net

Responsible Competitiveness in Arab World 2009. *Accountability.* London. Forstater, M., Zadek, S., Guang, Y., Yu. K., Hong, C. X. and George, M. (2010). Corporate Responsibility in African Development: Insights from an emerging Dialogue. *The Institute of West-Asian and African Studies of the Chinese Academy of Social Sciences,* Working paper No. 60.

6

International Bodies and Benchmarks of CSR

David Katamba and Charles Tushabomwe-Kazooba

6.1 INTRODUCTION

The concept of corporate social responsibility is indeed wide, and by this point we highly believe that the reader has come to appreciate its breadth. Due to its broadness, it has been given different dimensions, depending upon the way a given profession or person conceptualizes it (please refer to Chapter Two for details and for recommended articles and textbooks cited). However, various international bodies have been formed to harmonize this broadness without compromising the international importance of the CSR subject and practice. They have frequently attempted to achieve this by integrating new global/international issues that have yet to be addressed on a global/international level (which cannot be solved by involved companies or on a national level). The formation of these international bodies has also helped to address the interests of corporate social responsibility stakeholders as well as to make further gains in the significance of the concept.

Notable among the international bodies are the Global reporting Initiative (GRI), the UN Global Compact, the World Business Council for Sustainable Development (WBCSD), the Organization for Economic Cooperation and Development (OECD); and the International Organization for Standardization (ISO). While the previous chapters particularly Chapter Four and Five have tried to highlight the tools that some international bodies have developed, especially when it comes to Reporting and measurement of CSR, this chapter seeks to focus on important selected international bodies (UN Global Compact, WBCSD, GRI, OECD, and ISO).

CHAPTER OBJECTIVES AND LEARNING OUTCOMES:

At the end of this chapter, the reader should be able to:

1. Profile different international approaches and standards for corporate social responsibility
2. List the different international/global issues driving corporate social responsibility
3. Influence their company's acceptance of international corporate social responsibility related standards

LIST OF SUBTOPICS IN CHAPTER SIX:

This chapter covers the following subtopics:

1. The UN Global Compact
2. The Global Reporting Initiative
3. World Business Council for Sustainable Development
4. Organization of Economic Council and Development (OECD)
5. International Standards Organization (ISO)

6.2 THE UNITED NATIONS GLOBAL COMPACT

The UN Global Compact is a voluntary initiative, which was launched by the United Nations on July 26, 2000. The Compact seeks to promote responsible corporate citizenship so that business can be part of the solution to the challenges of globalization and help to realize a more sustainable and inclusive global economy. The international/global CSR issues that the UN Global Compact seeks to address are reflected in its "ten principles of the Global Compact." The January 2008 joint publication by the UN Global Compact and Office of the High Commissioner for Human Rights, entitled "Embedding human rights in business practice II" (p. 13), highlights these 10 principles. The principles are clustered into four themes as follows:

1. Human rights: Businesses should—Principle 1: Support and respect the protection of internationally proclaimed human rights. Principle 2: Make sure that they are not complicit in human rights abuses.

2. Labor standards: Businesses should uphold—Principle 3: Freedom of association and the effective recognition of the right to collective bargaining. Principle 4: The elimination of all forms of forced and compulsory labor. Principle 5: Effective abolition of child labor. Principle 6: The elimination of discrimination in respect of employment and occupation.

3. Environment: Businesses are asked to—Principle 7: Support a precautionary approach to environmental challenges. Principle 8: Undertake initiatives to promote greater environmental responsibility. Principle 9: Encourage the development and diffusion of environmentally friendly technologies).

4. Anticorruption:—Principle 10: Businesses should work against corruption in all its forms, including extortion and bribery.

From the above, we see that the UN Global Compact pursues four main CSR issues from a global/international perspective, that is, Human Rights, labor, environment and anti-corruption. However, they are not binding to any business entity but rather rely on public accountability, transparency, and the enlightened self-interest of companies, labor and civil society to employ and pursue these principles. Any company that finds the Compact's ten principles worthy of embrace has to sign up voluntarily with the UN Global Compact. It also has to makes a periodic "Communication of Progress" (COP) to the Global Compact showing its progress regarding adherence to the 10 principles. For details of how to register and get involved in the Global Compact's activities, kindly visit: http://www.unglobalcompact.org/

6.3 GLOBAL REPORTING INITIATIVE

Popularly known for its Sustainability Reporting Guidelines, the Global Reporting Initiative (GRI) is a multi-stakeholder initiative formed to develop globally applicable guidelines that can be used voluntarily by companies to disclose their intervention and contributions towards economic, environmental, and social issues. The Guidelines cover disclosure ranging from a company's strategy and management approach to its economic performance and market presence, materials, energy and water used, as well as emissions and waste produced. It incorporates labor practices and basic rights, involvement with the local community, as well as product responsibility, to provide a complete picture of company behavior. As highlighted in Chapter Four, the GRI provides various "Guidelines and indicators" that help companies to structure their disclosure through corporate social responsibility reports. The GRI also provides useful tools for strategic planning, which help companies to arrive at a comparable description of their economic, ecological and social contributions.

From the above, we find that the main international/global corporate social responsibility issue that the GRI pursues is "Disclosure" of the firm's impact. This disclosure centers on social, economic and environmental issues that surround a business. Application of GRI guidelines is voluntary. Therefore, a firm that wishes to benefit from GRI has to register voluntarily with GRI by visiting the GRI website (http://www.globalreporting.org/Home).

6.4 WORLD BUSINESS COUNCIL FOR SUSTAINABLE DEVELOPMENT

From the WBCSD website (http://www.wbcsd.org/), the World Business Council for Sustainable Development (WBCSD) is a CEO-led, global association of over 200 companies dealing exclusively with business and sustainable development. By the time of authoring this book, the WBCSD members come from more than 35 countries and 20 major industrial sectors like mining and minerals, forestry, mobility, tire industry, etc. The Council has a global network of over 60 national and regional business councils and regional partners.

Its identity dates back to the 1992 Rio Summit, with the efforts of Stephan Schmidheiny, a Swiss business entrepreneur. When he was appointed chief adviser for business and industry to the secretary general of the United Nations Conference on Environment and Development (UNCED), he created a forum which he branded the "Business Council for Sustainable Development." The actual name, WBCSD, was created in 1995, following a merger of the Business Council for Sustainable Development and the World Industry Council for the Environment. The Headquarters of WBCSD are in Geneva, Switzerland, but the council also has major offices in Washington, D.C., and Brussels, Belgium. The mission statement and objectives of WBCSD is outlined in Table 20.

WBCSD plays a catalyst role in encouraging business to buy into the concept of sustainable development and to change the way they run their operations. It also catalyzes the process of global policy

Table 20   WBCSD Mission Statement and Objectives

Mission Statement
To provide business leadership as a catalyst for change toward
sustainable development, and to support the business license to operate,
innovate and grow in a world increasingly shaped by sustainable
development issue.

The Council's objectives are to:
• Be a leading business advocate on sustainable development;
• Participate in policy development to create the right framework
conditions for business to make an effective contribution to sustainable
human progress;
• Develop and promote the business case for sustainable development;
• Demonstrate the business contribution to sustainable development
solutions and share leading edge practices among members;
• Contribute to a sustainable future for developing nations and nations in
transition.

development, through representing and promoting the role of business in achieving sustainable development. The Council provides a
platform for companies to explore sustainable development, share
knowledge, experiences and best practices, and to advocate business
positions on these issues in a variety of forums, working with governments, non-governmental and intergovernmental organizations.

6.5 ORGANIZATION FOR ECONOMIC CO-OPERATION AND DEVELOPMENT (OECD)

The OECD adopted its Declaration on International Investment
and Multinational Enterprises in 1976 to facilitate direct investment
among OECD members. As part of the latest review of the Declaration, in 2000, the OECD and its member nations jointly recommended to multinational enterprises operating in or from their
territories the observance of OECD Guidelines for Multinational
Enterprises. These constitute a comprehensive, multilaterally
endorsed code of conduct for multinational companies and provide
voluntary principles and pragmatic standards for responsible business
conduct in a variety of areas, including environment, human rights,
labor and industrial relations, and governance. The Guidelines for
Multinational Enterprises have since consolidated their position as
one of the world's principal instruments in the field of corporate
responsibility. Companies use the instrument as guidance to under-

stand their responsibilities and to formulate public commitments, or codes of conduct, in the countries in which they operate. The recommendations are made by 39 adhering governments, and while they are not binding, governments are committed to their observance. The OECD Guidelines and an annual report related to the initiative in French and English are available on-line (at www.oecd.org), along with the text of the broader Declaration on International Investment and Multinational Enterprises. PDF e-books or paper copies of these and related documents may be acquired from the OECD's online bookshop (at www.oecdbookshop.org). For more details, visit: www.oecd.org.

6.6 INTERNATIONAL ORGANIZATION FOR STANDARDIZATION

International Organization for Standardization (ISO) is an international body that offers a series of voluntary standards to help organizations meet the challenges of sustainable development and CSR. The standards that are set by ISO provide both a model for streamlining environmental management and guidelines to ensure that social, economic and environmental issues are considered within a decision-making framework. The ISO standard (ISO 26000) that particularly relates to CSR was in draft by the time (October 2010) of authoring this book. By then, ISO (in particular standard 26000) observed seven international/global CSR issues that have to be observed. These are: organizational governance; human rights, labor practices; the environment; fair operating practices; consumer issues; and lastly community involvement & development.

How to Benefit from the ISO

The ISO has CD-ROM containing over 20 published standards of the ISO family in a user-friendly configuration, along with related drafts nearing completion. With reference to CSR, The ISO deals with the principles and requirements for conducting and reporting life-cycle assessment studies in the seven focal areas: organizational governance; human rights, labor practices; the environment; fair operating practices; consumer issues; and lastly community involvement & development. The reader is therefore requested to visit the ISO website www.iso.org to check for details about the final draft of ISO 26000 standard which deals with CSR. A company that meets any standards set by ISO is certified with such a relevant standard. This standard gives it more credibility when competing both locally and globally. It is important to note that ISO certification guarantees to stakeholders that certain measures and systems are in place in such companies. However, certification is not a formal confirmation that these systems are adhered to consistently, year after year.

6.7 CONCLUSION

This chapter has not exhausted all the international bodies that have put their efforts into the development CSR. It has only surveyed the most commonly referenced international bodies—GRI, UN Global Compact, OECD, ISO and WBCSD. It has also attempted to show where and what each of them focuses on, as well as providing the readers with information that can be explored further so as to participate and benefit from any of these bodies.

6.8 LEARNING ASSIGNMENTS

1. Without being limited to the notable bodies discussed in this chapter, profile (in a tabular form or otherwise), the various international bodies relating to CSR, clearly highlighting how each body addresses the dimensions of CSR.
2. From the profile above, and with reasoning included, indicate which bodies or body you perceive to be the most relevant or comprehensive in addressing CSR aspects.

6.9 REFERENCES

Hunter, L. L. (2008). Rethinking Production. *In State of the World, 2008*, p. 34.

Laider-Kylander, N. (2004). *The World Business Council for Sustainable Development (WBCSD) Millennium Report.* http://fletcher.tufts.edu/netimpact/downloads/WBCSD_Laidler-KylanderApr04.pdf.

Appendix One

Organizations Actively Promoting the Development of Corporate Social Responsibility (CSR) in Uganda

1. Corporate Social Responsibility organizations

The Corporate Social Responsibility Consultative Group (U) Ltd: This is a network that brings together major CSR promoting agencies and stakeholders in Uganda. The Group's key activities are: CSR Training/Consultancy where it conducts research in CSR, organizing academic conferences, and developing a CSR Curriculum for Universities; CSR Knowledge Development whereby it promotes CSR in Uganda through conferences, workshops, dialogues and by recognition and awards for CSR best practices; and CSR Promotion/Recognition through which it offers CSR consultancy for implementation of strategic CSR and conduct CSR trainings for managers.

For details, please visit: www.csrconsultativegroup.com

Uganda Chapter for Corporate Social Responsibility Initiatives Ltd (UCCSRI): This is the leading not-for-profit private limited company in Uganda that provides CSR Information and advisory services. Its major objective is to promote and support the implementation of CSR that improves the competitiveness and market opportunities for companies, corporations, and small and medium enterprises (SMEs) operating in Uganda. As a company that has expertise and specialized knowledge, it provides guidance, and a platform and avenue to discuss and exchange corporate social responsibility ideas and sustainable development issues in Uganda. Currently, UCCSRI helps and coordinates companies and enterprises operating in Uganda to continuously embrace corporate Social responsibility and Sustainable Development issues across all their operations. It does this through the contribution of knowledge, research and development in corporate social responsibility issues, extension of skills and capacity building, as well as offering consultancy in the management of business processes to comply with CSR trends.

For details, please visit: www.uccsri.com

Email: info@uccsri.com

Corporate Social Responsibility Chainlink: The Corporate Social Responsibility Chain Link is a partnership of 3 organizations: the Danish Development Research Network (DDRN), Institute of Corporate Governance of Uganda (ICGU) and Uganda Christian University, Mukono (UCU). The CSR Chainlink promotes collaboration between researchers and experts of Corporate Social Responsibility (CSR), corporations and institutions involved in CSR, as well as community leaders. The CSR Chainlink aims to build on issues of CSR and Good Governance, and linking this to sustainable development by enabling socially responsible players to contribute towards social investment as a long term endeavor instead via on and off projects. Vision: Improving Corporate Social Responsibility deliverance to create sustainable development. Mission: Creating a link through stakeholders to improve access to Corporate Social Responsibility information for companies and the Ugandan people.

For details, please contact, Harriet Ssali (Esq) via email: harriet_ssali@yahoo.com

Ecolife-Uganda: This is a CSR service provider organization committed to promoting strategic CSR in particular and sustainable development in general, among the business community, academia, and the wider public. The Organization seeks to create 21st Century Business Leaders who are equipped with the vision and knowledge necessary to integrate corporate profitability with environmental and social considerations (values). Ecolife Uganda helps companies integrate strategic CSR within their operations, as well as contributing towards CSR knowledge development by promoting research, and by organizing academic conferences and lectures, among others.

For details, please contact: Mr. Hamid Tenywa on email: hamidhakim61@hotmail.com

2. DEVELOPMENT PARTNERS

Deutsche Gesellschaft für Internationale Zusammenarbeit (GIZ):

Working efficiently, effectively and in a spirit of partnership, we support people and societies in further development, and aid transitioning and industrialized countries in shaping their own futures and improving living conditions. This is what the Deutsche Gesellschaft für Internationale Zusammenarbeit (GIZ) GmbH is all about. Established on 1 January 2011, it brings together the long-standing expertise of the Deutscher Entwicklungsdienst (DED) gGmbH (German Development Service), the Deutsche Gesellschaft für Technische Zusammenarbeit (GTZ) GmbH (German technical cooperation) and Inwent—Capacity Building International, Germany. As a federally owned enterprise, we support the German Government in achieving its objectives in the field of international cooperation for sustainable development. GIZ is the official development partner and donor to the CSR Consultative Group (U) Ltd's activities. It also independently supports the members of the CSR Consultative Group, to run special CSR or PPP (Public Private Partnership) projects. Some members that have benefited from this include: UCCSRI, LEU, UMA, FUE, and others. It is also actively promoting the UN Global Compact's activities in Uganda through funding special activities to this cause.

For details, please visit: www.giz.de.

3. ACADEMIC INSTITUTIONS

Makerere University Business School (MUBS). This is the leading business school in Africa, popularly known for its vision, "the benchmark for business and management education in the region." MUBS has excelled at Business and management teaching and research. It offers market-oriented and demand-driven programs that bring graduates right to the center of the main events in world Business. The School teaches about business and how to manage it, even for those not inclined toward business; it offers management knowledge that enables individuals to succeed where they work. The School will help individuals achieve the dreams they set out to achieve. It has consistently made CSR related subjects part of its knowledge transfer to its students and clients.

For details please visit: www.mubs.ac.ug.

Kampala International University (KIU) is a fast growing private University in the region. The University is positioned towards responding to societal needs by designing and delivering an educational system guided by the principles and values of respect for society, economy, and environment. The University ensues that the educational experiences of students will result in productive graduates who can contribute positively to the overall well being of society. The KIU School of Business and Management is committed to promoting and integrating CSR in particular, and sustainability issues in general, within its curricula and activities. One of the seminal events for CSR promotion within the University is the annual KIU-Corporate Week.

For details please visit; www.kiu.ac.ug.

Mbarara University of Science and Technology (MUST), founded by the 1989 Act of Parliament, follows a Community Based Education [CBE] programme, as its underlying philosophy. Right from the start, community based problems make the focus of students' training in all the courses of the current four faculties and institutes. The University places great emphasis on CBE in recognition of the great need for professionals who are trained to deal with the needs of the society into consideration, professionals who are competent to implement strategies and other national policies, and have the right attitude towards the major problems of the country—rapid population growth, rising levels of poverty, unemployment, environmental degradation, natural disasters and health issues. Community Based Education programme as a philosophy is strongly linked to Corporate Social Responsibility in a number of ways. For instance, the university over the years has implemented a number of programmes in the communities. Among the programmes are business clinics, support to hospitals and health centres, sensitizations on health living, education programmes, sending health teams to villages, support to displaced persons, training village health workers, support to schools, providing basic health education, teaching - information, communication and Technology and gender sensitization in secondary schools, women, UPDF and Police, psychology to secondary school teachers on how to handle class, communities on some crop vermin sis. Furthermore, university curricula are continuously designed to incorporate social and environmental issues, components of corporate social responsibility. This means courses have relevance to policy of Uganda National Development Plan 2010–2014 for promoting good governance and sustainable development thus leading graduates of the university to create employment or to be employed.

Website: http://www.must.ac.ug

Gulu University. One of the new public universities in Uganda, Gulu University is located in northern region, an area which has been under political insurgency since 1987. Although its establishment had been planned in the early 1980s, it was only in 2002 that the university finally opened its doors to the public, four years before the official date of the end of the war.

The original title of Gulu University of Agriculture was later replaced with Gulu University, which was deemed to be more appropriate. Many stakeholders preferred the latter title because it gives the university flexibility to focus all-inclusive life challenges both in the natural sciences as well as the socio-economic arena.

Although at the moment there is no specific programme of study leading to academic qualifications in Corporate Social Responsibility (CSR), the concept is manifested in practical terms in two ways: research and outreach activities involving both students and faculty. In research, the Faculty of Agriculture and Environment, for example, is engaged in studies aimed at developing improved breeds of local animals and crops for the benefit of the communities. The Faculty of Medicine is engaged in research on mental health—which is currently a big problem in the post-conflict northern Uganda in general, and Acholi sub-region in particular. In the social sciences, there are also a number applied research projects in the areas of conflict management, especially involving local traditional principles and practices of justice as a means of building sustainable peace in the region. Engagements in human security are also manifested in studies focusing socioeconomic challenges of the communities. Students' internship projects and consultancies involving academics at the university also play a role by engaging members of the community and local governments in training in specific skills such as statistics, ICT, book-keeping, counseling, and a host of many others.

Thus CSR is a core value of Gulu University in line with its mission which is to play the lead role in community transformation in northern region and Uganda as a whole.

Website: http://www.gu.ac.ug/

4. NON-GOVERNMENTAL ORGANIZATIONS

Living Earth Uganda (LEU): LEU has been working in Uganda for over a decade and was formally established as a Ugandan NGO in September 1999. This environmental and developmental NGO is a partner of the Living Earth Foundation, UK. Objectives: to Support poor urban communities in practically addressing environmental issues in their local areas. LEU works with government, communities and the private sector to promote environmental education and to facilitate partnership formation between stakeholders in environmental management and education. It also promotes policies, practices and strategies that will ensure proper environment and natural resource management in Uganda. LEU's Mission is to "strengthen the capacity of communities and individuals to improve their local environment and economic welfare, by increasing their levels of knowledge, awareness and skills in environmental management and helping them translate these ideas and skills into action."

For details please contact: www.livingearthuganda.org.

5. GOVERNANCE ORGANIZATIONS

The Institute of Corporate Governance of Uganda: The Institute of Corporate Governance of Uganda (ICGU) is a not-for-profit membership-based organization established in Uganda to foster the corporate governance values of account-ability, transparency, integrity and responsibility. The Institute derives its mandate from the Memorandum and Articles of Association and it is governed by an 11-member Council and a Secretariat headed by a Chief Executive Officer. Vision: An enterprise sector that upholds international best practices in corporate governance. Mission: To promote excellence in corporate governance principles and practices. Its core activities include conducting and coordinating corporate governance training for Directors and Senior Management to enhance board and management performance, with better understanding of duties and responsibilities for the benefit of all stakeholders. It also publishes and disseminates information on Corporate Governance through public awareness lectures, pamphlets, discussion papers, the Institute Journal and other documents associated with the affairs and activities of the Institute and other associated agencies.

For more information, please visit: www.icgu.or.ug.

Lucky Family Business, Ltd™ (LFB™) was established in 2005 and is mandated to offer consultation to family-based business entities. LFB™ has an edge in its solid consultancy team of experts in the Family Business field. The LFB™ team has researched and published extensively in the area of business. Some of the works include the bestselling book, "Comprehensive Guide on Family Business Governance" (2005), "Trust" (2007), and "Boil Your Head" (2009), with many more works including research papers, business cases, and conference papers (both regional and international). LFB™ has recently organized more than five international Family business conferences. LFB™ has a strong regional network in the Southern Sudan, Uganda, Kenya and Tanzania. LFB™ works in association with a number of policy-making bodies, including the Private Sector Foundation of Uganda, the Uganda Manufacturing Association, the Institute of Corporate Governance of Uganda, the Kenya Institute of Management, the Uganda Chamber of Commerce and Industry, the Uganda Chapter of Corporate Social Responsibility Initiatives, the Makerere University Business School, as well as many other business institutions and pivotal family business personalities in East Africa.

For details, visit www.luckyfamily.biz.

6. MANUFACTURER ASSOCIATIONS

Uganda Manufacturers Association (UMA): This is the largest organization representing the broad industrial and commercial sectors of Uganda's economy, and an important forum for the private sector in the country. UMA has a membership comprising nearly 750 small, medium and large enterprises drawn from both the private and public sector. Vision: To be among the most valued and respected business association worldwide serving the interest of its members, shaping national and regional policies and leading the industrial sector towards sustainable global competitiveness. Mission: To promote and protect the interests of industrialists and manufacturers in Uganda. Goals and Objectives: To promote, protect and coordinate the interests of industrialists in Uganda; to act as a watchdog and an effective mouthpiece for its members; to initiate discussions and an exchange of information amongst members on industrial issues; and, to advise the Government on key policies affecting industry.

For details, please visit: www.uma.or.ug.

Index